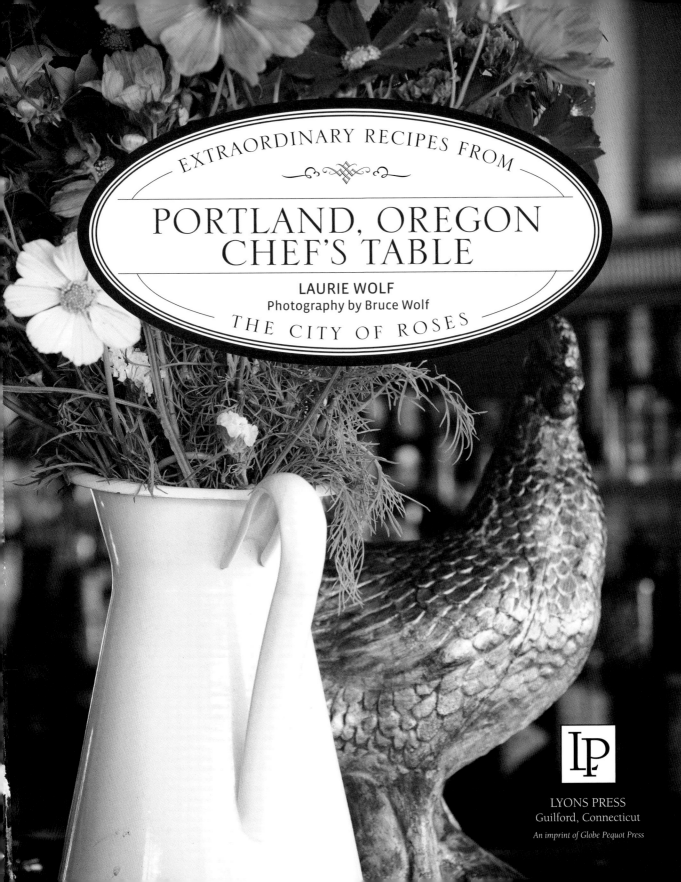

EXTRAORDINARY RECIPES FROM

PORTLAND, OREGON
CHEF'S TABLE

LAURIE WOLF

Photography by Bruce Wolf

THE CITY OF ROSES

LYONS PRESS
Guilford, Connecticut

An imprint of Globe Pequot Press

To buy books in quantity for corporate use
or incentives, call **(800) 962-0973**
or e-mail **premiums@GlobePequot.com.**

Lyons Press is an imprint of Globe Pequot Press.

All interior photos by Bruce Wolf unless otherwise noted.

Project editor: David Legere
Text design: Elizabeth Kingsbury
Layout: Nancy Freeborn

Library of Congress Cataloging-in-Publication Data is available on file.

ISBN 978-0-7627-7810-2

Printed in the United States of America

10 9 8 7 6 5 4 3 2 1

Restaurants and chefs often come and go, and menus are ever-changing.
We recommend you call ahead to obtain current information before
visiting any of the establishments in this book.

For Nick, who has put up with my challenges moving into the age of technology with kindness and humor, maybe not in that order.

For my husband, Bruce, it seems like both a week and an eternity that we have known each other. Thanks for all the good times and good photos.

And to Olivia, who is the person in my life who has stretched me the most, whose determination and bravery have changed my parenting philosophy over and over again. She is an amazing, challenging, and joyous addition to all our lives. There is no stopping her: She is an inspiration.

CONTENTS

Soups

Brunch

Sandwiches

Large Plates

Desserts & Pastries

Acknowledgments

For someone who feels about cooking and dining the way I do, this book has been perhaps the perfect project. It has allowed me to explore the food scene here in Portland in great depth, seeing the restaurants during the nonpublic times of day—during the deliveries, the setting up of the tables, the bread slicing—and the personalities of all the people who come together and make these extraordinary restaurants possible. We photographed during the weeks leading up to the James Beard awards, when there was a buzz of excitement and nerves. We were in the kitchens the days when the word got out that some favorite haunts had closed and when new places had their soft openings. During a very chilly and rainy May, we were there to hear talk of how the weather needed to change to get the tables outside, and when it would be warm enough to start getting the local berries that rule the summer menus.

Portland is a very manageable city. It is easy to get around; there is little traffic; and there are few people, if any, who are too busy to give an interview or to help carry equipment from the car to the restaurant. And as insignificant as it may sound, we have been able to park in front of every restaurant we photographed.

This book is filled with over a hundred terrific recipes. All of the chefs have been incredibly generous with the dishes they have allowed me to include. I did not expect to get the crust from Random Order, the matzo ball soup from Mother's, or the sugo from Caffe Mingo. I could go on. I am deeply indebted to every restaurant and shop we visited, where everyone from the head chef to the people washing the dishes was helpful, warm, and hospitable. I envy all of these people in the kitchens and farms; they are in the middle of something huge and wonderful.

Writing this book has made me a different—and I think better—chef. I love that. I hope that everyone who owns a copy of *Portland, Oregon Chef's Table* puts it to frequent use, lets it get a little food stained, and even turns back some corners. My favorite cookbooks are the ones that get the most worn, which is how it should be.

My editor at Globe Pequot, Katie Benoit, might possibly be the nicest and most upbeat person in the world. She is brilliant at saying what she wants and responding with such warmth and positive energy that I want to give her the best book in the world. And to Janice Goldklang, who has made this whole thing possible, a thousand thanks for your kindness and humor.

To thank everyone who helped, I would need to include a list of hundreds of names. There are, however, some people who gave extra time, advice, and expertise and clearly need to get an individual shout-out. For Andy Ricker and Kurt Huffman, many thanks for the suggestions and the door openings. For the guys at Victory Bar, Yoni Laos and Eric Moore, you made things ever more delightful and delicious. Bette Sinclair offered a wealth of information and helped us connect with a host of places. Bruce Carey gave us his time and his firsthand knowledge of the history of the PDX food scene. Same goes to Michael Cronin, who was a wealth of knowledge and city lore. Jenn Louis and David Welch, of Lincoln and Sunshine Tavern, were always ready to help and were nourishing spiritually as well as culinarily. Gabriel Rucker was patient and adorable when Bruce photographed him cooking during actual service in his tiny gem of a restaurant, Le Pigeon. Megan Henzel of Roost and Tracy Olson of Random Order provided much needed sustenance during this delicious journey. John Taboada of Navarre and his lovely wife, Giovanna, shared with us some great restaurant suggestions, as well as smart and interesting stories filling out the Portland food scene. Dayna McErlean and her son Bishop made our trips to their amazing world of wonderful Yakuza energy, beauty, and food fun.

To all the farmers and ranchers, winemakers (special thanks to Ron and Lynn Penner-Ash) and beer brewers, bread bakers and kitchen cleaners, suppliers of everything food-related, thank you for being willing to do the very hard work, setting an example throughout this country of your commitment and dedication despite not always getting the kudos you deserve. To my friends Freddi Greenberg, Ellen Shea, and Pam Abrams, thank you for your help and support and for being willing to read something over "just one more time" when I was feeling creatively challenged or insecure. To the Ovist family, you have no idea how much I needed "Mallory." And if you are lucky, you will get to observe one of Ms. Yeomen's fun demos at one of the local Farmer's Markets.

In addition to the professional shout-outs, there are family members and friends who need to be graciously thanked. First, my husband, Bruce, who is capable of taking such great photographs that I never have to give it a thought. He is patient, has a great eye, and has knowledge of food and drink that makes him a valuable contributor in more than just the realm of photography. My children, Nick and Olivia, are so happy that we are happy, getting to work and live in this phenomenal city that we have come to love dearly. Thanks to Fred and Geri Goldrich, for always being supportive and willing to listen to me go on and on about an amazing piece of brisket or slice of pie. To event planner extraordinaire Marcy Blum, much appreciation for fifty-something years of wit, wisdom, and friendship. Gold.

We have lots of friends who have gone with us on our dining adventures, enabling us to order way more than we could have alone and not be mortified. The Micks, Parkins, Mendons, Parker/Hirschfelds, Hubbards, Kristen and Leslie, and the always entertaining Nichols family (Judy, John, Katie, Jack, and the lovely Madge) were great sports and game to try anything. Well, almost anything. (You know who you are.)

Finally, to John and Janet Jay, the people we followed to Portland. Close friends and unsurpassable dining companions, thanks for everything. When I think about how old "the boys" are, I smile, remembering hanging out with you, over twenty years ago, the last two women in The Calhoun Schools lunchroom while our three-year-olds adjusted to academic life. Love you all.

Introduction

When I started work on this book, it seemed pretty straightforward. Eat again at all the places I had eaten previously, and go to all the others. Enjoy something immensely, and the next day contact the chef and arrange for it to be photographed for the book. Living in Portland as a food lover is a daily adventure, between the farmers' markets, when the spring arrives, and the bakeries, taverns, and restaurants, all year-round.

There is, however, another component that is fascinating and, I think, extremely important, in a socioeconomic, environmental, globally conscious way. It's this: People live differently in Portland. I am constantly reminded of the quirky TV show on IFC, *Portlandia*, a hilarious series that is set in and pokes gentle fun at our city. Comedian and writer Fred Armisen says to his friend, Carrie Brownstein, guitarist from the now-defunct band Sleater-Kinney, "Portland is where young people go to retire." Although clearly that's an exaggeration, in humor there is often truth, and this is no exception, because Portland is a vibrant and creative community where people (of all ages, actually) often relocate to explore a different and more relaxed way of life.

While writing this book, I have interviewed over seventy-five people—chefs, bartenders, restaurant owners, and perhaps most important, farmers. It seems to me that the people who chose to live in Portland, whether raised here or from out of town, have made a life choice, a choice that is mostly based on being attracted to the freedom of the casual, balanced Portland lifestyle.

This lifestyle is reflected in the way Portlanders dress. In fact, the majority of diners feel comfortable in shorts. I can only think of three restaurants that might frown on that, but I'm not sure that's the case.

This casual vibe, however, in no way implies that food—or the dedication of the food community—is taken any less seriously in PDX (the way we refer to Portland). What it does bring to the picture is a lack of fussiness and pretension in the way food is cooked and presented. Particularly with the younger chefs, there is a driving movement to keep the food simple, relying on the freshest and highest quality products and preparing them in the way that allows the ingredients to shine.

The farm-to-table movement is clearly guiding the food community. Chefs deal directly with the farmers, and the results are farm fresh. There are eggs on a lot of things. Perhaps the egg is the mascot of the farm-to-table movement. (Or is it the chicken? I'm not sure which came first.) In addition to the cutting-edge food scene, this is a very exciting time in PDX because the farm-to-table movement represents a movement back to community, and to solidarity, and to taking care of people who in turn give something back.

It started out, in my head, that this was going to be a book about food. And of course, with over one hundred recipes, it is, but the political and sociological implications of this food movement are huge. This may, quite possibly, be the beginning of a shift in America, a renewed appreciation for the place where you live, the people who provide all the services, and the importance of heeding the warnings we have been given about protecting this planet.

When interviewing the owners of Victory Bar, Yoni Laos and Eric Moore, Laos made a comment that seems right on. The food movement, he said, is not unlike an indie music scene. Members come together to form a band, work on something for a while, then move on, start other bands, go solo, and so on. It seems like a good comparison, this group of young, hip, smart people creating tantalizing food and sharing tremendous camaraderie, vision, product, and friendship.

Because the focus of the food movement here is farm-to-table, all of the chefs work with local farmers and ranchers, and what is in the restaurant on any given day is what was in the ground, on the tree, or grazing the day before. This is why the food is as intense as it is, which makes a huge difference in how it tastes. It is not unusual to see the best-known chefs in town at any of the ten or so farmers' markets each week. It is this integrity that makes the product the highest priority, along with the people responsible for getting the goods to your table.

This movement's roots in seasonality also means that all restaurant kitchens will inevitably receive most of the same product delivered daily—asparagus in April and May, raspberries in June and July, and lamb in the spring, for example. And, because there are lots of chickens in Portland, there are lots of eggs, and they show up in unexpected places, like on the top of an amazing Monte Cristo at Sunshine Tavern, or in a mind-boggling Kentucky Hot Brown, a great brunch dish, at Roost.

What becomes one of the challenging parts of this philosophy, and what draws the chefs together yet also sets them apart, is how wide a range of creativity exists with the ingredients available. During its month-long peak, asparagus, for example, turned up in soups, on sandwiches, battered and fried, under a fried egg, and on a million burgers, but—I am pleased to say—never in a dessert. For the most part, use of all of these seasonal products makes for creativity without the food becoming silly or pretentious.

Some years ago, when I was a chef in Manhattan, we received our eggs, dairy and produce from a little farm in upstate New York. We wouldn't know exactly what we would get, and sometimes it was just five heads of an unusual lettuce that would show up on a Monday morning. It was one of the best parts of the job. Since Mondays were on the slow side, that would be the day of the week when we would brainstorm, some of us with cookbooks in hand, others with a new spice or a jar of "first time available in the States" preserved lemons.

I can completely understand why the chefs here are stoked. They get to be constantly creative; they live in a part of the country that offers an enormous bounty of products and possibilities. And the possibilities are seemingly endless: Within an hour of Portland, you can be at a world-class winery; exploring orchards of cherries, pears, and peaches; at a cheese maker producing phenomenal product; or picking vegetables at one of the area's hundreds of farms.

By the time you read this, some of the restaurants included here will have closed, the victims of an uncertain restaurant economy or our ever-changing cravings. Some of the chefs may be cooking in new kitchens, as protégés graduate from their mentors and masters experiment with new cuisines. No matter. Large or small, steady or fleeting, universally popular or critically praised—these restaurants and chefs have shaped how we eat.

The recipes and cooking insights the city's chefs have generously provided here ensure that you can always go back for seconds even as the menu of the Portland restaurant scene continues to evolve.

Small Plates

Since it is clear that this book needs to reflect the full scope of the PDX food scene, I have chosen to refer to what would normally be called first courses at restaurants and cafes as "small plates." There are, I guess, subtle differences, but often people will construct their entire meal from these tasty but less filling starters. This style of eating offers greater variety, and often chefs seem to take this opportunity to be a little more inventive, or even daring. It's a smaller commitment and a great opportunity to be adventurous—for both the chef and the diner.

For years this kind of eating was popular in certain ethnic cuisines, such as the Spanish tapas and the Japanese izakaya. It's a meal that can be a simple journey or a culinary exploration, with the perfect balance of salty and spicy, subtle and outrageous. Chef John Taboada of Navarre (see page 160), for example, offers a menu that he puts together himself, allowing his expertise to take you on an interesting food journey. And the wonderful Asian restaurant Ping, one of Chef Andy Ricker's places, offers mostly small plates, with standout dishes like quail eggs, hard boiled and wrapped in bacon and sauced.

It is still possible, of course, to start off with a simple mixed green salad. The greens will be fresh as can be and the dressing interesting, though it is hard not to try several of the unusual and at times remarkable small plates.

CLYDE COMMON

1014 SOUTHWEST STARK STREET
(503) 228-3333
WWW.CLYDECOMMON.COM
CHEF: CHRIS DIMINNO
OWNER: NATE TILDEN

Clyde Common is one of Portland's hot spots. Connected to the ultra-hip Ace Hotel, it is one of the few west-side haunts that draw as many young, tattooed hipsters as it does the more expected, not so edgy, west-side crowd. Both the bar and the dining room are always packed, and the communal tables allow for easy mingling and fun. Upstairs there are small tables for groups of two or four, and it lends itself to more quiet and privacy. The cookbook-papered walls on both levels are a lovely touch.

Chef Chris DiMinno, the charming Culinary Institute of America–trained chef from Westchester, New York, sets the friendly and mellow tone for the open kitchen, which sends out food that is sophisticated and amusing. Clyde Common is a low-key place, full of young über-cool people, and they are eating studied-yet-casual food in a room with a definite buzz. There is almost a clublike atmosphere in the main dining room, and either the same people go all the time and they really do know each other, or they just act that way. Portland is a small town, and on occasion you can go to one of these hot spots and run into half the people you know.

Clyde Common is a well-located restaurant for attracting both locals and out-of-towners. There is no way someone staying at the Ace can avoid eating a meal or two there, and Portlanders know that this is a place to get a great pour and a good meal, then head over to Powell's or the Living Room Theatre to keep the mood going.

The menu is fun, with starters like spiced popcorn and fried chicken wings with pomegranate and orange, and large plates of standout dishes like sturgeon, Manila clams, fennel, and baby carrots in a prosciutto broth, or grilled steak Romesco (almond, garlic, and roasted pepper-scented puree) with spring onions and a spicy arugula salad. Seasonal is the name of the game here, with the chef working with local farmers and purveyors to keep everything in the community.

The vegetable salad is especially good. The ingredients depend on what's currently available. You can choose from asparagus, tomatoes, corn, peppers, and mushrooms, among other things. The sky is the limit. The key is to make sure you have a wide variety of vegetables, both raw and cooked, and vary as many cooking techniques as possible: braised onions, grilled asparagus, raw bok choy, blanched snap peas, and so on. This salad is as delicious as it is beautiful, with the truffle cream an outstanding accompaniment to the just-picked veg.

Truffled Seasonal Vegetable Salad

(SERVES 4–6)

For the truffle cream:

2 cups plain whole milk yogurt
1 teaspoon kosher salt
Cracked black pepper
1 tablespoon good-quality honey
1 tablespoon black truffle oil

Suggestions for the salad:

5 baby carrots, peeled, cleaned, and blanched
½ cup cauliflower florets, tossed in olive oil,
    and roasted in the oven
½ of a Granny Smith apple, peeled, diced,
    and roasted in a baking pan
½ cup broccoli florets, blanched in salt water
2 baby radishes, sliced thin on a mandoline
4 tablespoons olive oil
4 teaspoons lemon juice
2 teaspoons white balsamic vinegar
½ teaspoon salt
A few grinds of fresh white pepper
Greens and herbs for garnish
Olive oil and sea salt to taste

Special equipment: Cheesecloth

Remove the yogurt from the container and place in a cheesecloth bag. Allow the yogurt to hang in the refrigerator overnight, over a bowl.

The next day, discard the drained water. Remove the yogurt from the bag and put in a stainless mixing bowl. Whisk in the salt, pepper, honey, and truffle oil. Set aside.

To finish: Spoon a decent amount of the yogurt onto each plate. Place all of the vegetables in a bowl and reseason with olive oil, lemon juice, white balsamic vinegar, salt, and pepper. Layer the vegetables in an attractive fashion, and garnish with your choice of greens and herbs. Finish the dish with more good-quality olive oil and flaky sea salt.

TRUFFLE HUNTING IN THE FOREST

Having grown up in the Bronx, there was not much opportunity to forage for truffles. My experience was limited to a few magical moments having fresh truffles shaved on my pasta in Italy and using truffle oil and truffle salt in my home kitchen. I love the taste, the smell, and the way that the flavor explodes when combined with cream, butter, cheese—all the fats that make truffles come alive. Truffles are easiest thought of as mushrooms that grow underground. The similarity ends there, though, because they do not have a root system like mushrooms.

Jack Czarnecki, the former owner of the Joel Palmer House in Dayton, Oregon (now owned by his son Chris), knows plenty about truffles. He graduated from Andover and UC Davis with a degree in bacteriology. While at Davis he studied under Dr. Maynard Amerine in the Department of Viniculture and Enology. Jack has written three books on mushroom and truffle cookery, including *A Cook's Book of Mushrooms,* which won the James Beard award in 1996. Several years ago he began experimenting with producing truffle oil from native Oregon truffles. As a result, his oil is the first in the United States to be produced all naturally.

Truffle oil is the best way to get the truffle taste experience. That's because fats have an affinity for those aromatic gases, so while you eat something enhanced by the truffle oil, you get a much stronger taste of the truffles.

Truffle oil is very delicate, and the gases that provide the flavor are driven off very quickly by heat. Therefore, never use the oil for the actual cooking preparation but rather as a finishing and flavoring oil. Here are recipes for truffles:

TRUFFLED BUTTER

(MAKES OVER 1 CUP)

You will need a 1-quart plastic container with a tight-fitting lid for this recipe. A glass jar with a tight-fitting lid will also work.

1½ ounces very ripe Oregon white truffles, sliced
½ pound butter, either salted or unsalted

Place the truffles at the bottom of a 1-quart plastic container. Place the butter over the truffles but not touching the truffles. You can do this by laying a small piece of wax paper on top of the truffles, allowing enough air space for the truffle gas to circulate. Place the lid on the container and allow it to sit in the open at room temperature for 2 hours. Refrigerate the container for 3 days.

After 3 days remove the truffles and use the butter for sauces, soups, and so on. If the truffles are still fairly firm and dry, they can be placed over your finished dish.

TRUFFLED CHEESE

You will need a 1-quart plastic container with a tight-fitting lid for this. A glass jar with a tight-fitting lid will also work.

1 ounce Oregon white truffles, sliced
14 ounces mild cheese, such as Gouda

Place the truffles at the bottom of a 1-quart plastic container. Place the cheese over the truffles but not touching the truffles. You can do this by laying a small piece of wax paper on top of the truffles, allowing enough air space for the truffle gas to circulate. Place the lid on the container and allow it to sit in the open at room temperature for 2 hours. Refrigerate the container for 3 days.

After 3 days remove the truffles and use the cheese for sauces, soups, and so on. If the truffles are still fairly firm and dry, they can be placed over your finished dish.

TRUFFLED CREAM CHEESE

You will need a 1-quart plastic container with a tight-fitting lid for this. A glass jar with a tight-fitting lid will also work.

1 ounce Oregon white truffles, sliced
12 ounces plain cream cheese

Place the truffles at the bottom of a 1-quart plastic container. Place the cheese over the truffles but not touching the truffles. You can do this by laying a small piece of wax paper on top of the truffles, allowing enough air space for the truffle gas to circulate. Place the lid on the container and allow it to sit in the open at room temperature for 2 hours. Refrigerate the container for 3 days.

After 3 days remove the truffles and use the cheese for spreads, dips, and so on. If the truffles are still fairly firm and dry, they can be placed over your finished dish.

PARK KITCHEN

422 NORTHWEST 8TH AVENUE
(503) 223-7275
WWW.PARKKITCHEN.COM
CHEF-OWNER: SCOTT DOLICH
CHEF DE CUISINE: DAVID PADBERG

Park Kitchen is one of the Portland restaurants that are strictly bound by the seasons. Scott Dolich and David Padberg want to serve food that reflects its surroundings and have over the years developed close relationships with local farmers and ranchers. The menu is small but generally well thought out, and there are always a number of options that will please the pickiest of diners. The restaurant's location, close to the Pearl and downtown Portland, is across from a small but lovely green space, and on a nice day it is possible to sit outside and watch people playing bocce or just enjoying the sun and sky. Dolich set the scene for the wonderful food at Park Kitchen, a directive that Padberg executes on a daily basis.

Padberg is renowned for unusual pairings of food combinations, and although I have hesitated on a couple of occasions, he has not let me down. Not unlike Le Pigeon's chef, Gabe Rucker, Padberg seems to have a sixth sense of how things will taste together, and I have had some stunningly unpredictable dishes that blew me away. The menu features small and large plates, allowing for lots of tastes without a commitment to an entree-size portion. During the summer, I sampled crispy duck blini with peas and lavender,

followed by magnificent Chinook salmon with caraway and cucumbers. My husband, Bruce, enjoyed his pork three ways, and our daughter, Olivia, surprised us all by ordering and loving a carpaccio of halibut, zucchini, and basil. And recently I enjoyed razor clams marinated with blood oranges and celery. The short ribs are perfection, and the lamb cassoulet is as good as anything France has to offer.

Desserts are always excellent, a recent favorite being the sesame date cake (although it was a toss-up between that and the flavorful and refreshing grapefruit-tarragon sorbet with crispy anise cookies). Cocktails are on par with the food, and the selection of wines and before- and after-dinner drinks is generous. The staff is knowledgeable about every part of the menu, as well as friendly, professional, and there when you need them.

Flank Steak Salad with Blue Cheese

(SERVES 2)

For the vinaigrette:

2 tablespoons plus ¾ cup canola oil
1 medium shallot, peeled
½ cup dry sherry
½ cup sherry vinegar
¾ cup olive oil
Salt and pepper to taste

For the sherry onions:

1 red onion
½ cup dry sherry
½ cup sherry vinegar
8 ounces flank steak, thinly sliced cooked rare to
    medium rare
2 ounces crumbled blue cheese
2 ounces sherry onions (see recipe below)
24 parsley leaves
6 red leaf lettuce leaves

Prepare the vinaigrette: Preheat oven to 325°F. In a hot sauté pan, add 2 tablespoons of canola oil and start the caramelization of the shallot on all sides, then deglaze with a small splash of dry sherry. Place the sauté pan in the oven for about 35 to 45 minutes until tender.

In a blender combine sherry vinegar, ¾ cup canola oil, olive oil, salt, and pepper. Puree until smooth, and adjust the desired thickness with water.

Prepare the sherry onions: Slice the red onion in half from the root to top, leaving the skins on. In a casserole dish, lay the onion sliced side down, and pour into the dish the dry sherry and sherry vinegar. Roast for about 45 minutes until firm but yielding, not soft and mushy.

Remove from the oven and cool, then peel the onion, removing the root end, and slice into strips.

To finish: In a medium bowl combine the steak, blue cheese, sherry onions, parsley, and lettuce leaves. Toss with the shallot vinaigrette. Divide among two plates.

Biwa

215 Southeast 9th Avenue
(503) 239-8830
www.biwarestaurant.com
Owner: Gabe Rosen
Chef: Ed Ross

Originally from Des Moines, Iowa, Chef Gabe Rosen opened his lovely and popular izakaya in March 2007, offering a large menu with small items. This low-key restaurant serves food that attempts to replicate the dishes eaten by a typical Japanese family. The food in Japan is greatly influenced by other cultures, mainly China, Korea, and the West. Rosen suggests that although Japanese cuisine is guided by the season, there are staples that are always available and comprise a large portion of the cuisine. Kimchee is made daily, and the process is fascinating to watch. It is flavorful and spicy and a great complement to many of the menu offerings.

Chef Rosen is drawn to Japanese culture, and at twenty-five he received a degree in Japanese studies from Portland State University. The restaurant is decked out in light woods and interesting art, and the design is the work of his business partner, architect Kina Voelz. Biwa is a great place to try lots of foods. The aged ashi tofu is fabulous and the gyoza among the best I've had. The grilled items are first rate, personal favorites being the scallop and the pork belly. The udon and ramen are the real thing, and there is a large selection of shochu and sake. The restaurant stays open late, and it is a terrific place to get a bite or two after a movie or PDX event. Biwa is Japanese comfort food, and after a meal there you leave feeling sated and healthy. That's nice.

Hiya Yakko

(SERVES 2)

For the sauce:

1 cup soy sauce

1 small piece konbu seaweed

2 tablespoons grated ginger

Small pinch of katsuobushi (dried shaved bonito flakes)

1 block silken tofu

1 tablespoon grated ginger

3 tablespoons thin sliced green onion tops

¼ cup katsuobushi

Combine the sauce ingredients and let sit in the refrigerator overnight.

Cut the tofu block into thirds, and cut the thirds into 4 cubes. Place the cubes in a shallow bowl or on a plate. Drizzle with the sauce and garnish with grated ginger, green onion, and katsuobushi.

Note: This dish is very simple and a great warm weather treat—not to mention a classic Japanese preparation and a good introduction to tofu.

Kinpira

(SERVES 2)

1 medium carrot, peeled
1 burdock root, peeled
2 tablespoons vegetable oil
2 tablespoons sake
2 tablespoons soy sauce
1 tablespoon sugar
1 teaspoon toasted sesame seeds

Cut the carrot and burdock into matchsticks. Heat the oil in a pan. Add the vegetables and stir-fry over high heat about 3 minutes or until the vegetables begin to soften.

Add the sake, soy sauce, and sugar. Stir well and cook over high heat until the liquid is almost completely reduced. Serve hot or at room temperature sprinkled with sesame seeds. This dish keeps well for up to a week in a covered container, and it is great as a starter or a side to any meat, chicken, or fish dish.

PING

102 NORTHWEST 4TH AVENUE
(503) 229-7464
WWW.PINGPDX.COM
CHEF: ANDY RICKER
OWNERS: JOHN AND JANET JAY AND KURT HUFFMAN

Ping, located in the Old Town/Chinatown neighborhood, offers Vietnamese and Thai street food in a warm and intimate setting. The narrow room with its wood-planked walls and collection of old radios makes diners feel as though the restaurant has been there for years. Tables are covered with laminated Asian newsprint, and a light fixture, designed by Seattle artist Yuri Kinoshita, distributes a warm and welcoming glow across flowing white fabric above the kitchen counter, where diners can sit on comfortable, sleek stools.

Ping is the sister restaurant of the venerable Pok Pok (see page 128), and Chef Andy Ricker, who oversees his many places, has traveled through Asia extensively and earned countless awards for all of his eateries. The food at Ping nourishes the soul—heady soups and noodle dishes, skewers of grilled meat and chicken, and quail eggs wrapped in bacon and drizzled with a Russian dressing-like sauce that is pure heaven.

Like the Japanese izakaya, Ping is the place to go to order lots of different foods, along with house-made drinking vinegars that are now available for purchase at Ricker's restaurants.

Ping offers interesting cocktails and thirst-quenching beers, which help to wash down some of the delicious and fiery hot house-roasted peanuts or amazingly tasty and mouth-burning spicy boar collar. During our visit the giant roasted pork knuckle brought stares and gasps as it made its way to our table. This is an out-of-this-world dish, but best to order it when you are with at least four people or when you want to bring the leftovers home and create some magic of your own.

Ping is one of the pioneers in the neighborhood that is undergoing a huge gentrification. There is a strong movement to bring new life into this faded part of town—new restaurants and markets and an Asian-style youth hostel, a joint venture by realtor David Gold, Alex Calderwood from the Ace hotels, and Portland power couple John and Janet Jay.

Carrot Cake

(SERVES 2)

This two-part recipe is a bit time consuming but well worth it. Baking the radish cake first and freezing what you don't use makes it much easier the next time. Just defrost and go.

For the radish cake:

2 pounds daikon radish, peeled and grated, squeezed until relatively dry
2 tablespoons vegetable oil
3½ cups water
2 cups rice flour
1 teaspoon ground white pepper
2 teaspoons kosher salt

2 tablespoons vegetable oil
1 7-ounce portion of radish cake
1 tablespoon thinly sliced garlic
½ cup white onion, julienned lengthwise
½ cup bean sprouts
2 extra large eggs, beaten
½ ounce Kecap Manis (sweet dark soy sauce from Malaysia)
½ ounce light soy sauce
¼ cup chopped green onions
Few dashes of white pepper
1 tablespoon torn cilantro

In a sauté pan, fry the daikon in the vegetable oil for 5 minutes. Add 1 cup of water, bring to boil, and cook for 15 minutes until soft. Drain.

Mix the rice flour and remaining water together to make a slurry. Add daikon to slurry, mix well, turn into oiled square aluminum pan, and steam over high heat for 10 to 15 minutes or until set.

Cool in refrigerator uncovered. When completely cooled, cut the radish cake into 1-inch squares. Divide into 6 7-ounce portions. Freeze unused portions of the daikon cake.

Heat the oil in a nonstick skillet. Fry the radish cake until golden brown. Add garlic and onion and fry for 1 minute. Add the bean sprouts and continue cooking. Add the eggs and cook until set.

Add the Kecap Manis, soy sauce, green onions, and white pepper. Mix, turn onto a medium plate, and sprinkle with the torn cilantro.

Natural Selection

3033 Northeast Alberta Street
(503) 288-5883
WWW.NATURALSELECTION.COM
CHEF AND OWNER: AARON WOO

For about two years in college I was a vegetarian. I gave away my leather bags and shoes and attended every PETA rally in the city. I lived on steamed vegetables and brown rice, and although in those days choices were pretty limited, food was merely sustenance and a political stance.

When my interests turned to the food industry, and I attended a two-year program at the Culinary Institute of America, it felt impossible to continue this life choice. I have never stopped attending PETA meetings, but I now eat animals of all kinds and their parts and don't feel hypocritical.

Dining at Natural Selection, a vegan and vegetarian restaurant on Northeast Alberta Street, I could imagine eating that way again. There is nothing the least bit predictable or boring about the offerings. Every course is meticulously prepared and presented in masterful combinations of thrilling tastes and textures.

Although not a vegetarian himself, Chef Aaron Woo wanted to offer superb food for the noncarnivores, who are often limited to the same vegetables and rice I was eating daily many years ago. Chef Woo's warm and even temperament is reflected in the serenity of his restaurant, the style of the food, and the decor, all of which are conducive to a special evening of relaxation. The menu is deliberately limited; in fact, there are four courses, each with only two choices, and each dish is more beautiful and sensual than the next. Not for one moment did I yearn for a piece of beef or miss the ubiquitous chicken breast—under, over, or in the middle of anything.

The food is delicate yet satisfying. It seems that you can taste every meticulously chosen ingredient, and the flavors are never overpowering; rather, they work in harmony, and the experience is astoundingly fabulous. Before going to dinner, I had anticipated a possible after-dinner stop for a venison burger, but when the meal was over, getting a burger was the last thing on my mind. I left feeling impressed, sated, and happy.

ROASTED PEACHES, FIGS, FETA & SALSA VERDE

(SERVES 8)

2 ripe peaches, each quartered—8 total wedges
½ teaspoon fennel pollen or ground fennel seed
¼ teaspoon ground coriander seed
1/8 teaspoon paprika
½ teaspoon lemon zest
1/8 teaspoon sea salt
Pinch of black pepper
1 tablespoon extra-virgin olive oil
2 tablespoons agave syrup or honey
8 (1-inch) chunks of feta cheese
1 tablespoon minced shallot
1 teaspoon lemon zest
Sea salt to taste
Black pepper to taste

1 tablespoon lemon juice
3 tablespoons extra-virgin olive oil
1 tablespoon chopped parsley
1 tablespoon chopped mint
1 tablespoon chopped tarragon
1 tablespoon chopped fennel frond
1 tablespoon minced chives
8 ripe Black Mission figs, each fig sliced
    into three rounds
2 tablespoons white balsamic vinegar
Pinch of sea salt
1 cup frisée lettuce or other lettuce of choice,
    portioned into 8 equal parts
4 tablespoons hazelnuts, toasted and crushed

Preheat the oven to 400°F. In an 8-inch sauté pan on medium heat, toast the fennel pollen, coriander, and paprika until just fragrant, about 1 minute.

Add the lemon zest, sea salt, and black pepper, then the extra-virgin olive oil, and cook for 1 minute. Add the agave syrup; cook for 1 more minute to blend well. Add the peaches and toss gently to coat evenly.

Using a fork, turn the peach wedges so that the skin side is down in the sauté pan. Put the sauté pan with peaches into the 400°F oven and roast until golden, about 4 minutes. Remove the peaches from the oven and place a chunk of feta cheese onto each peach wedge. Turn off the oven, then put the peaches back into the oven to warm the feta cheese.

In a small bowl combine the shallots, lemon zest, sea salt, black pepper, and lemon juice. Let stand for 5 minutes. Add the extra-virgin olive oil to the bowl and mix well. Add all of the chopped and minced herbs and gently stir to combine. Adjust seasoning as desired.

Toss the sliced figs with the white balsamic vinegar and sea salt. Place the figs in a circle on the center of a plate. Put a portion of frisée onto the sliced figs. Place a wedge of roasted peach and feta cheese onto the frisée. Spoon some of the salsa verde onto the peach and onto the frisée or plate.

Top with the toasted crushed hazelnuts and serve.

FARMERS' MARKETS

The Portland Farmers Market was established in 1992 by three founders: Craig Mosbaek, Ted Snider, and Richard Hagan. These local activists worked with local farmers who wanted to supply fresh produce, meats, and prepared goods to the people of PDX. The original market had thirteen vendors on opening day, and then grew to twenty-two that first year. Shortly after that, the main Saturday market moved to the PSU campus, and a second market was added on Wednesdays in 1997.

Each year the number of vendors has grown and today there are over 250 vendors, selling their goods at six different PDX locations. The Saturday market at PSU is huge, and you could spend hours shopping, eating, listening to live music, and talking with the farmers and other purveyors.

Evoe

3735 Hawthorne Boulevard
(503) 232-1010
www.pastaworks.com
Head Chef: Kevin Gibson
Owner: Peter Garmo

Eating at Evoe is an adventure in simplicity and brilliance. The restaurant is part of Pasta Works, a terrific gourmet shop on Portland's east side. The dining area consists of a few tables and some seats at the counter in front of the tiny, open kitchen showcasing an oven, a couple of griddles, and some cold storage areas. Every dish is done to order, with the choices listed on the blackboard above the cooking area.

Chef Gibson has the cooking cred that puts him up with the best in town. He grew up in Iowa in a family where each of the four kids had to make dinner one night every week. He quickly developed a passion for food and cooking and moved to Portland, where he attended the Western Culinary Institute. He worked in some of the most highly regarded eating places in town—Genoa for four years before opening Castagna, where he served as chef for eight years. He is a master at creating simple combinations of the highest quality products and taking them to a level that is hard to live up to. Genius.

The cooking in France, Italy, and Spain predominantly inspires the menu at Evoe. The place is a monument to food creativity. The sandwiches are outstanding, my personal favorite—at the moment—being the Dansk, made with house-cured gravlax. The calamari and chickpeas, baked in a spicy aioli, is killer, and the Sauvie Island beet salad is the best beet treatment I have had. Being a founding member of the deviled egg fan club, I was momentarily reborn after tasting the stuffed-and-then-griddled version of this dish that simply cannot be improved on. I went back, just for the eggs, three times that first week.

SQUASH CARPACCIO

(SERVES 6)

1 butternut squash, peeled and seeded
12 tablespoons balsamic vinegar
¼ cup pepito seeds, toasted
12 mint leaves, chopped
Coarse salt

Slice the squash as thinly as possible. A mandoline would be perfect, though you can also use a vegetable peeler. Use the whole squash.

Distribute the squash among 6 plates, piling it up and making it look as graceful as possible. Drizzle each pile with balsamic vinegar, and top with the toasted seeds. Sprinkle with the chopped mint and salt.

DEVILED EGGS

(SERVES 6)

6 large eggs, hardboiled and peeled
¼ cup mayonnaise
2 teaspoons freshly grated horseradish
1 teaspoon Dijon mustard
1 teaspoon champagne vinegar
Salt and black pepper to taste
2 tablespoons melted butter
½ cup brioche crumbs

Carefully cut the eggs in half, removing the yolks and placing them in a small bowl. Set the egg white cavities aside. Add the mayonnaise, horseradish, mustard, vinegar, salt, and pepper to the egg yolks and mix well. The mixture should be smooth and creamy. If you prefer, you can puree in a food processor for a perfectly smooth yolk mixture.

Fill the egg white cavities with the yolk mixture, pressing down gently.

Dip the stuffed eggs into the melted butter, filling side down, then into the brioche crumbs.

Place the eggs, crumb side down, in a nonstick skillet. Cook until golden brown. Serve warm.

FOOD CARTS

It seems like the number of food carts in Portland varies depending on whom you ask. I have heard estimates from 200 to 700, and according to the PDX Food Carts website, the count is hovering around 600. There is a great turnover, some carts closing for the winter, some due to illness and some, happily, closing their carts to open a "real" restaurant. The carts are spread around the city, some sitting in a field by themselves, while others are in groups, called pods, with up to twelve different trucks in one location.

I cannot think of a cuisine that is not represented. Because they are simpler to open and close, the mix changes frequently. Some are open early in the day only, while others don't open till the late afternoon, and stay open well past midnight. The quality of the food is impressive considering it comes out of the back of a van or truck. The food can be quite ambitious, and the prices are considerably less than at a traditional restaurant.

LAURELHURST MARKET

3155 EAST BURNSIDE STREET
(503) 206-3097
WWW.LAURELHURSTMARKET.COM
EXECUTIVE CHEF: DAVID KREIFELS
CHEF DE CUISINE: PAULINE DRUMM
OWNERS: DAVID KREIFELS, BEN DYER, AND JASON OWENS

Laurelhurst Market is a local favorite. It is always packed, with folks at the bar enjoying top-of-the-line cocktail offerings and super fun food off the standing rail menu. Executive Chef David Kreifels works on making the most of what is available at the local farms and farmers' markets, making sure that the dishes that accompany the beef or pork reflect the same high standards. Bartender Eric Nelson worked in kitchens before he took his place behind the bar. He takes his cocktails seriously, expecting from them the same high standards he had for his food. Watching him make the house tonic water is fascinating, from the muddling of the lemongrass to finding its home in a superb gin concoction.

The food at Laurelhurst is meatcentric, although the restaurant serves some of the best mussels and clams in town. The chalkboard hanging from the ceiling shows the cuts of beef and what is available on any particular night. The edamame-style fava beans are crazy good, and so is the *suppli al telefono* (short rib and mozzarella risotto fritters). The beef is top rate, and there are unusual cuts, teres major for one, that is tender and tasty like a filet mignon but considerably less pricey. The braised pork shank is aromatic and tender, and the marrowbones starter is a great use of that now-in-fashion food, with a vinegary dressing of parsley, pickled shallot, and fried capers that cut the overdose of fat that can be problematic if not prepared properly.

Laurelhurst Market's butcher shop, which sells top-quality sausages, pâtés, and rillettes, all done in-house, is a must experience. The well-priced meats and poultry are all interesting cuts from local ranchers. While there, don't pass on one of the Market's sandwiches, featuring all house-cooked and cured meats with nothing but the best produce, bread, and the restaurant's "special sauce." I go for number three every time, called simply the Ham and Salami—what a great sandwich.

Roasted Marrowbones with Basil Pistou, Pickled Shallots, Capers & Toast

(SERVES 6)

18 (3-inch) marrowbones, cut lengthwise

For the pickled shallots:

½ cup sugar
½ cup champagne vinegar
¼ cup water
1 sprig thyme
1 bay leaf
A few peppercorns
Pinch of salt
2 cups peeled shallots

For the pistou:

3–4 garlic cloves
1 bunch fresh basil, roughly chopped
Pinch of salt
½ cup mild olive oil or a mix of ¼ cup each
   canola oil and extra-virgin olive oil

For the garnish:

12 pieces sourdough bread or other white bread
Few sprigs parsley
Handful of capers
Fleur de sel
6 tablespoons pickled shallots
Salt and pepper to taste

Soak bones, cut lengthwise (no more than 3 inches long), in salted water in the refrigerator overnight. Before serving, remove bones and let air-dry for a half hour.

Preheat the oven to 425°F.

Roast the bones in the preheated oven until a toothpick can be inserted in the marrow with only slight resistance, about 10 minutes.

In a medium saucepot combine the sugar, vinegar, water, thyme, bay leaf, peppercorns, and salt. Bring the mixture to a boil, check for flavor, then pour over peeled and thinly sliced shallots. Allow to cool to room temperature. Store in refrigerator.

Prepare the pistou: Bring 2 cups of water to the boil and add garlic, blanching for 2 to 3 minutes to remove the raw heat. Allow to cool.

In a mortar and pestle, smash garlic with a little salt, then add basil with a little of the oil. Smash until a paste begins to form. Gradually add more oil and process as you go. Season with salt and pepper to taste.

To finish: Toast 12 pieces of sourdough or other mild white bread. (The bread is just a vehicle to carry the marrow and shouldn't be a prominent flavor.)

Place the bread alongside the marrowbones and drizzle lightly with the pistou.

Garnish the plate with some pickled shallots, a few sprigs of parsley, and a few capers. Finally, hit the marrowbones with just a touch of fleur de sel.

LINCOLN

3808 NORTH WILLIAMS STREET
(503) 289-0120
WWW.LINCOLNPDX.COM
CHEF AND OWNERS: JENN LOUIS AND
DAVID WELCH

Lincoln is turning out some of the most outstanding food in Portland. The almost five-year-old restaurant seats about seventy guests in this airy and open corner spot on North Williams Street. The place is beautifully designed, with steel-clad walls in the open kitchen, lots of glass and light wood, and a huge charcoal drawing of a rooster on a brick red wall. It's stunning.

Jenn Louis trained at the Western Culinary Institute and worked in restaurants around town for several years, including a stint at Wildwood, where she met her future husband, David Welch. Jenn, being a chef, and David, being a front-of-the-house guy, combined their careers and in 2008 opened Lincoln.

The food at Lincoln is modern, with Italian influences and a significant Northwest sensibility, and the menu changes regularly to reflect the products that are seasonal and at the peak of flavor and ripeness. Hen eggs baked with cream, Castelvetrano olives, and herbed bread crumbs is brilliant; fresh burrata (the creamy cousin to mozzarella) with Detroit red beets, almonds, and Maldon salt is a superb example of Louis's exceptional talent for ingredient pairing; and another winning dish, roasted pork belly with a panzanella of morel mushrooms, garlic, and sage—tender and tasty—is the entree everyone fights over.

GRILLED OCTOPUS, LINCOLN-STYLE

(SERVES 6 AS A FIRST COURSE)

1 cup white wine
½ lemon, sliced into ⅛-inch disks,
    ends and seeds discarded
1 teaspoon black peppercorns
2 dried bay leaves
1 tablespoon kosher salt
1 cup cold water
3 pounds octopus, cleaned

For the octopus:

6 plus 3 tablespoons olive oil
3 tablespoons sherry vinegar
1½ tablespoons pimentón (Spanish paprika)
Kosher salt
Freshly ground black pepper
Octopus, tentacles and head separated into 8 pieces

Special equipment: Outdoor grill

For the salad:

6 tablespoons olive oil
3 tablespoons red wine vinegar
8 ounces baby lettuce leaves
1 large shallot, sliced thinly
4 ounces shaved fennel bulb
10 Castelvetrano olives, pitted and cut into thirds
Kosher salt
Freshly ground black pepper

In a large pot, combine wine, lemon slices, peppercorns, bay leaves, and salt. Add 1 cup cold water. Place cleaned, rinsed octopus into the pot, adding enough water to cover completely. Weight octopus with a ceramic plate or bowl to keep below the surface of the water bath.

Place the pot over high heat and bring to barely a simmer. Steam should rise from the pot, but

bubbles should not be present. Cook for 4 hours, covered with only the ceramic plate. Remove the octopus from the pot and cool to room temperature before proceeding.

To make the octopus: Whisk together 6 tablespoons olive oil, sherry vinegar, pimentón, salt, and pepper and set aside. Rub 3 tablespoons olive oil on the octopus and grill over hot coals, until octopus is warm, moist, and slightly charred on outside. Cut octopus tentacles into 1- to 2-inch chunks and toss in vinaigrette.

To make the salad: Whisk together olive oil and red wine vinegar. Toss lettuce leaves with shallot, fennel, and olive pieces and season with salt and pepper. Drizzle enough dressing to gently coat the greens. Divide on 6 plates. Lay octopus pieces on the greens.

ANDINA

1314 NORTHWEST GLISAN STREET
(503) 228-9535
WWW.ANDINARESTAURANT.COM
CHEF: HANK COSTELLO
OWNER: PLATT RODRIGUEZ FAMILY

Andina, located in the upscale Pearl neighborhood, serves the best Peruvian food in Portland. It is a popular spot for celebrations, both on date night and with groups of friends or business associates. There are always people toasting something, and there are lots of fun libations to aid in the festive mood. Caipirinhas are made the way they should be, as are the mojitos and the wonderfully tart, refreshing, and powerful pisco sours.

Chef Costello was raised in Oakland with a mom who was a pastry chef. He grew up cooking and made his living in college working in kitchens. When college was done, he decided to go the culinary route. Costello's first experiences in fine cuisine began in the Castilla region of Spain, where he learned from family members the essence of true Spanish gastronomy. With ten years' training in the culinary arts, Costello's "Spanish connections" contribute to the impact of his work at Andina.

The menu at Andina is long, with lots of choices in every category, especially the starters. You might prefer to dine there in a group to sample many shared *entradas.* The ceviches are all very good, but a personal favorite is the green mango with passion fruit and prawns. The potato cakes (*causa*), particularly the green bean and cheese, taste so good that you might want to get two if you are a largeish group. Piquillo peppers are stuffed with cheese, quinoa, and Serrano ham, and empanadas are as good as they get—flaky pastry stuffed with tender beef, raisins, and olives. The lamb shank, slow-cooked in the traditional northern Peruvian style with cilantro and black beer, is one of Andina's best entrees, although the wild mountain mushrooms wok-fried with onions, tomato sauce, garlic, and ají Amarillo peppers runs a very close second.

Desserts are just about impossible to pass up, with two of the standouts being the crisp quinoa-studded cannolis stuffed with passion fruit mousse and served with mango-lemongrass sorbet and caramel, and the creamy goat cheese and lemon cake served with fresh seasonal berries laced with basil and habañero, an unusual combo that works like magic. From start to finish, Costello serves up food that is unusual and definitely worthy of celebration.

Piquillos Rellenos con Chimichurri de Rocoto y Rábano

STUFFED SWEET PIQUILLO PEPPERS IN A GARLICKY VINAIGRETTE WITH PEPPERS AND RADISH

(SERVES 4)

For the chimichurri:

1 tablespoon deveined and finely chopped rocoto pepper (Peruvian hot pepper)*

2 tablespoons finely diced radish

1 ounce red wine vinegar

3 tablespoons chiffonaded cilantro

6 tablespoons chiffonaded Italian parsley

2 tablespoons finely chopped fresh oregano

6 ounces extra-virgin olive oil

1 tablespoon minced garlic

½ tablespoon kosher salt

Can substitute any spicy pepper

For the stuffed piquillo:

2 quarts water

½ pound white quinoa

½ pound black quinoa

2 tablespoons olive oil

1 tablespoon minced garlic

1 cup diced yellow onion

1 pinch ground cumin

1 teaspoon kosher salt

1 teaspoon ground black pepper

3 tablespoon ají amarillo puree*

¼ cup diced red bell pepper

¼ cup diced green bell pepper

6 carrots diced, blanched

2 tablespoons diced Serrano ham

1 large egg, lightly beaten

3 tablespoons diced Cotija cheese

1 tablespoon white vinegar

8 piquillo peppers, seeded and cleaned

If ají amarillo puree is unavailable, substitute other chile puree or chile paste (taste for spiciness)

Prepare the chimichurri: Mix all the items together in a bowl. Let sit for 2 hours as the flavors mature.

Prepare the stuffed piquillo: Divide the 2 quarts of water between two pots. Bring water in both pots to a boil; add white quinoa to one pot and black quinoa to other. Cook quinoa until al dente. (The black quinoa takes a little longer to cook.) Strain the quinoa from both pots. Run cold water through the quinoa to cool and then reserve.

Bring the oil to a medium heat in a sauté pan. Add the garlic until it browns. Add the onion, cumin, salt, and pepper. Once the onion is translucent, add the ají amarillo puree and cook for 5 minutes. Add peppers, blanched carrots, and Serrano ham. Cook for 5 minutes, stirring occasionally. Remove the mixture to a large bowl and let cool.

Once the mixture is cool, add salt to taste. Add the egg to the mixture and mix well. Mix in quinoa, vinegar, and cheese. Carefully stuff the piquillo peppers until the stuffing reaches the top of the peppers.

Place the stuffed peppers on a microwave-safe plate. Microwave for 2 minutes on high. Let sit for 1 minute. Top with the chimichurri and serve.

Pisco Sour

There is no place better than Andina for interesting south-of-the-border libations. Bartender Greg Hoitsma makes a pisco sour that's almost magical.

3 tablespoons pisco puro (Peruvian brandy)
2 tablespoons fresh-squeezed lime juice
2 tablespoons water
Baker's sugar to taste
1 teaspoon egg whites
Squeeze of lime juice
Dash of Angostura bitters

Shake pisco puro, lime juice, water, sugar, and egg whites without ice in a cocktail shaker. Add ice, then shake again to chill. Strain into a martini glass. Finish with a squeeze of lime juice, then a dash of Angostura bitters.

A TALE OF TWO PEPPERS

Dishes at Andina feature many ingredients that are not available in this country. Although Chef Costello wants to use ingredients that are local, it isn't always possible. Costello has, however, worked with several local farms willing to grow a couple of pepper varieties not previously grown in the Northwest. Two different peppers, the rocoto and the ají amarillo, are grown here specifically for Andina. The rocoto is grown at Gails Meadow Farm. The ají amarillo is grown on a small piece of land near the city. Very romantic. Very PDX.

Le Pigeon

738 East Burnside Street
(503) 546-8796
www.lepigeon.com
Chef and Owner: Gabriel Rucker

Le Pigeon is probably the smallest, and possibly the finest, restaurant in Portland. This tiny corner on East Burnside is the stage on which James Beard award winner Gabriel Rucker takes the simplest ingredients and turns them into stunning combinations of tastes and textures.

The restaurant takes reservations, and it's very busy, but it always leaves room at the kitchen-fronted counter for walk-ins who start appearing before the 5:00 p.m. opening time. On a typical evening, there are three chefs working the line. They are a talented bunch who appreciate and take great pride in being part of this extraordinary spot and are serious about maintaining its stellar reputation.

Chef Rucker is young and tattooed, and he's a huge baseball fan. He is generous with his time and knowledge and well respected in the food community with his well-

balanced and interesting menu, generally knocking it all out of the park. All ingredients on the menu are top quality, coming in fresh from local ranches and farms daily.

Sitting at the chef's counter watching the action is like being at a dinner theater without having to suffer through the mediocre performance. There is excitement in the air, everyone is totally pumped, and the magic begins. On a recent visit we dined on fabulously prepared snails served with orzo, cauliflower, and Parmesan and enjoyed the gnocchi with pheasant and seasonal parsnips. The veal marsala was perhaps better than that found in even the finest Italian restaurants. Bruce went for the burger—awesome.

Desserts are noteworthy, and Chef Rucker's signature dish, the foie gras ice cream–stuffed profiterole, is famous around town. It is impressive how well these combinations work together. It is a brave and brilliant mind who came up with this bizarre yet delicious offering.

GARLIC ROASTED ASPARAGUS WITH CROUTONS & MANCHEGO

(SERVES 4–6)

For the asparagus:

1 bunch asparagus
3 cloves chopped garlic
1 tablespoon extra-virgin olive oil
Zest of 1 lemon
Salt and pepper to taste

For the vinaigrette:

1 shallot, minced
2 tablespoons sherry vinegar
⅓ cup extra-virgin olive oil
Salt and pepper to taste

For the croutons:

2 cups focaccia cut into ½-inch cubes
3 tablespoons melted butter
½ teaspoon garlic powder
½ teaspoon paprika
Salt to taste
Chunk of Manchego cheese

Prepare the asparagus: Preheat the oven to 375°F. Trim the asparagus of woody bottoms. Toss all the asparagus ingredients together and roast on a baking tray for 7 to 8 minutes in the oven.

Prepare the vinaigrette: Whisk all ingredients together.

Prepare the croutons: Toss all ingredients together and bake in preheated oven for 6 or 7 minutes, or until crispy.

To serve: Lay the asparagus on a platter. Top with croutons and drizzle with vinaigrette. Shave fresh Manchego on top.

DOVE VIVI

2727 NORTHEAST GLISAN STREET
(503) 239-4444
WWW.DOVEVIVIPIZZA.COM
CHEF AND OWNERS: DELANE AND DEVON BLACKSTOCK

When I heard about Dove Vivi from Gabe Rosen from Biwa, I was told not to think of it as a pizza place, although it is, and not to have any preconceived ideas of what the pizza should taste like, though I did. This small, friendly restaurant, owned by delightful and talented husband and wife Delane and Devon Blackstock, is creating some amazing dishes, with brilliant pizza toppings and great salads at reasonable prices.

The couple learned pizza making from their mentor, Mike Freeman, who worked for years in San Francisco under the leadership of Patricia Unterman. Their version most resembles the deep-dish pizza from Chicago, although the remarkable crust at Dove Vivi is in a class by itself, made with organic cornmeal (from Bob's Red Mill), sustainably grown flour, and pure olive oil. Making the crust is painstaking and requires practice to get it right, but once it is right, it's unforgettable. At the restaurant, the crusts are partially prebaked, and the pans sit on shelves waiting to be topped and turned into magic.

The ingredients are locally sourced, and everything is made fresh daily, the toppings reflecting what is at the point of ripened perfection. In addition to the pizzas, the salads at Dove Vivi are unusual, change with the seasons, and stay true to the restaurant's dedication to, as Delane puts it, "the loot of our locale."

KALE SALAD

(SERVES 8–10)

For the dressing: (Makes about 1 cup)

⅔ cup extra-virgin olive oil

⅓ cup finely hand-chopped shallots (this is important, as food processors can cause shallots to taste too oniony in this delicate dressing)

Scant ¼ cup fresh lemon juice

½ teaspoon kosher salt

½ teaspoon freshly ground black pepper

For the salad:

3 bunches of Italian kale

2 ounces ricotta salata, shredded

In a medium bowl add all of the dressing ingredients and whisk to combine.

Wash the kale leaves and shake to remove excess moisture. Remove the stalks from the leaves and discard. Lay the leaves in stacks, several deep, and roll together. Shave off the ends with a knife to produce long, thin strips of kale. Combine in a large bowl and toss with the ricotta salata. Pour the dressing and the cheese on the greens, then toss thoroughly with tongs to combine well.

COCOTTE

2930 NORTHEAST KILLINGSWORTH STREET
(503) 227-2669
WWW.COCOTTEPDX.COM
CHEFS AND OWNERS: KAT LIEBMAN AND ZOE HACKETT

This lovely corner restaurant is in good company, sharing the street with PDX favorites Beast, Yakuza, DOC, and Autentica. The two women running the kitchen, Kat Liebman and Zoe Hackett, prepare French-bistro-meets-the-Northwest bounty using spectacular ingredients and a constantly changing seasonal menu. The food is delicate yet full of flavor and style. The space is intimate and romantic, decorated in an interesting combo of earthy and pretty. Botanicals line the pale walls, there is a handmade herb garden on the wall, and beautiful French doors open to views of this fun and trendy neighborhood.

Liebman and Hackett work their magic behind a curtained kitchen window while Hackett's husband, Levi, mixes creative and powerful drinks at the bar. Levi is charming and interesting, and eating at the bar is a lovely experience.

The chefs met during overlapping positions working at the elegant and pricey

restaurant Lucy's Table, which closed in 2011. In the entrepreneurial spirit of Portland, they decided to go off on their own and open a place that would allow their French culinary artistry to shine. Cocotte opened during a time that welcomed several "French"-inspired dining places in town. The *poulet en cocotte,* a milk-fed, confit-fried half chicken—and the dish that the restaurant is named for—is an excellent representation. The creamy chicken liver mousse is paired with a berry jam and some crisp and flavorful house-made pickles. And the Cocotte escargot bourguignon feature the snails in a velvety Mornay sauce with leeks and thinly sliced French bread. Very nice.

The impressive array of desserts continues the French theme paired with the Northwest bounty. The dense and rich flourless chocolate cake is served with whipped crème fraîche and candied Oregon hazelnuts and pairs well with an after-dinner drink. I suggest you linger over the fromage blanc, an Alsatian specialty, a spectacular French cheese cake with a shortbread foundation and filled with a not-too-sweet mix of white cheese, eggs, cream, sugar, and a hint of lemon.

SALMON MOUSSE PARFAIT

(SERVES 8–10)

1 pound salmon (can be smoked or fresh,
    depending on what you have available
    or what flavor you prefer)
6 cups heavy whipping cream
1 bunch basil or any herb that you prefer (tarragon,
    chives, or thyme would each work well)
1 teaspoon white wine vinegar
Pinch of kosher salt
Fresh ground black pepper
¼ teaspoon unflavored gelatin powder

Bring a large pot of water to a simmer and steep the ingredients (use 4 cups of heavy cream) for about 1 hour, until all of the flavor is in the cream. Transfer the cream and the steeping ingredients to a blender and blend until very smooth (do this in batches to avoid a mess). Pass the mixture through a fine-mesh sieve and set aside to cool to room temperature. Taste the mixture to be sure it has enough salt and acidity. Remember that it will be served cold and will be diluted by adding whipped cream, so this base flavor should be fairly intense.

In the bowl of a standing mixer, whip the remaining 2 cups of cream to soft peaks. Store in the refrigerator until needed. When the salmon/cream base has cooled to room temperature, fold in the plain whipped cream until the mixture is homogenous. Put the mixture in a container and store in the refrigerator to chill.

The mousse should set for at least a few hours before serving. It can be made a day or two in advance.

DOC Restaurant

5519 Northeast 30th Avenue
(503) 946-8592
www.DOCpdx.com
Owner: Dayna McErlean
Co-Chefs: Jobie Bailey and Paul Losch

This twenty-something-seat restaurant is a relative newcomer in the Concordia neighborhood. One of the more recent areas experiencing rapid gentrification, this two-block span is home to several of Portland's best eating places. DOC is in very good company, within shouting distance from Yakuza, Beast, Cocotte, and Autentica. With representation of totally different ethnicities and styles, the fact that these places are bunched together is pretty sweet.

DOC is an absolutely charming restaurant, designed by its owner, Dayna McErlean, whose eclectic, sophisticated, and sometimes playful style has created something unusual and quite special. To enter the dining room, patrons walk through the small kitchen. It's different, but it works, making you feel like you are in someone's home rather than a restaurant.

The kitchen takes up about a third of this restaurant's space. Jobie Bailey and Paul Losch, the two talented chefs, turn out remarkably good Italian-meets-Northwest cuisine, with careful attention paid to every detail; there is the sense that these dishes are just as they should be, beautifully paired ingredients at the height of their potential. Bailey got his start at the helm of the wonderful Pix restaurant, turning out some of the best brunches in Portland, while Losch received his formal training at London's Vong, cooking under Jean-Georges Vongerichten, and at the Culinary Institute of America in Hyde Park, New York.

Both the squash carpaccio and the risotto with snap peas, nasturtium, and chives are masterful, and the Swiss chard and porcini lasagna, topped with a perfectly fried egg, is one of the most divine dishes I have ever had. The flavors and textures combine to form the perfect plate.

Desserts should not be missed; particularly outstanding is the espresso panna cotta, served with crunchy always-changing biscotti. This small-but-mighty place to dine is serving dishes that are extremely delicate yet full of powerful pairings of the freshest food.

Dungeness Crab, Fennel & Cantaloupe Salad

(SERVES 4)

12 ounces Dungeness crabmeat

2 fennel bulbs, medium heads

½ cantaloupe, peeled and seeded

¼ cup roasted lemon vinaigrette (see recipe below)

2 tablespoons chopped chives

¼ teaspoon Controne chile flakes
   (or similar hot pepper flakes)

½ teaspoon lemon juice

Coarse sea salt to taste

Extra-virgin olive oil

Herbs for garnish (mint, basil, salad burnet)

For the roasted lemon vinaigrette:

1 lemon

1 tablespoon plus ¼ cup extra-virgin olive oil

½ teaspoon plus ½ teaspoon kosher salt

¼ teaspoon ground black pepper

½ cup lovage leaves

1 egg yolk

2 tablespoons lemon juice

¼ teaspoon Controne chile flakes

½ cup grapeseed or other neutral oil

Ice cubes or cold water as needed

Drain and squeeze the moisture from the crabmeat. Pick through the crabmeat to remove any pieces of shell or debris that may have been left from processing and place the crab in a medium-size mixing bowl.

Using a mandoline slicer or sharp knife, slice the fennel paper-thin. If using a large head of fennel, remove the core first. Adjust the mandoline to about 1/16-inch thick and slice the cantaloupe lengthwise. Reserve the cantaloupe for plating.

Combine the fennel with the crab, vinaigrette, chives, chile flakes, lemon juice, and salt. Taste and adjust seasoning if needed.

Divide the cantaloupe between four plates, spreading out into thin folds, and sprinkle with a little sea salt. Spread the crab over the melon, sprinkle with sea salt, and drizzle with olive oil. The salad can be garnished with mint, basil, salad burnet, or other complementary herb.

To make the vinagrette: Preheat the oven to 375°F and place a sheet pan or cookie sheet in to heat. Split the lemon in half lengthwise; remove the center pith and all seeds. Slice the lemon into ⅛-inch-thick half wheels. In a small bowl toss the lemon with 1 tablespoon olive oil, ½ teaspoon salt, and black pepper. Pour contents of bowl onto the hot sheet pan. Roast for 8 to 10 minutes, stirring occasionally, until the lemon is soft and slightly charred. Remove from the oven and allow to cool to room temperature, approximately 10 minutes.

In a blender combine the roasted lemon, lovage, egg yolk, lemon juice, chile flakes, ½ teaspoon salt, and one small ice cube. Puree on low until a paste is formed.

Once a paste has formed, with the blender still running, begin drizzling in ¼ cup olive oil. Once all the olive oil has been absorbed and emulsified, begin adding the grapeseed oil. After the first ½ cup, turn off the blender and taste the dressing. Adjust the seasoning as necessary, and if the dressing is still too acidic, turn the blender on and add more oil, 1 to 2 tablespoons at a time, until the dressing becomes creamy. It should have the consistency of a thin mayonnaise. If the blender is having a hard time turning the dressing, turn the speed up and adjust the thickness of the dressing with cold water, or add more ice cubes.

Rum Club

720 Southeast Sandy Boulevard
(503) 467-2469
www.rumclubpdx.com
Owners: Mike Shea and Kevin Ludwig
Bar Manager: Mike Shea
Chef: Ben Bettinger

With retro wallpaper, beautiful wood and tile on the curved bar, and outdoor seating, Rum Club is one of the coolest, most fun bars in Portland and just a great, funky place to hang. The atmosphere generates good times. It's dark and cozy, and you feel as if you are in some decked out basement from the '70s, more like you're at a private club than a bar open to the public. The bar splits the building and some staff with Beaker and Flask (see page 40) sharing the kitchen brilliance with the wonderfully talented and adorable chef Ben Bettinger.

Rum Club attracts chefs and bartenders from some of Portland's best known eateries and taverns. It is open until the wee hours, packing in the crowds throughout the night. The drinks are absolutely fantastic, potent, and a blast from the past. Rum rules here, but there is no problem getting a perfect vodka-, tequila-, or bourbon-based drink. My favorite rum-based drinks are the Rum Club Daiquiri and the Fawn Hall, prepared with Flor de Caña Rum 2x, Campari, Bonal, and an orange twist. The Exes and Ohs drink, a blackstrap rum with hints of vanilla and nutmeg, is also memorable.

Beyond drinks, the menu features some very cool snacks and sandwiches. The shrimp cocktail and the mussels and clams hit the spot on a rainy Portland night. The beautiful pickled eggs are spiced just right, and the egg salad sandwich with bacon and jam is just delish. I got a sampling of the deviled ham, and my bite was way too small. The drinks are really strong, so I suggest showing up at Rum Club with a thirst, an appetite, and a designated driver.

TURMERIC PICKLED EGGS

(SERVES 12)

1 dozen eggs
1 tablespoon salt
1 tablespoon olive oil
1 small onion, small dice
1 tablespoon turmeric
½ tablespoon red pepper flakes
½ cup white wine
1 cup champagne vinegar
½ cup water
¼ cup sugar
2 tablespoons salt
1 small bunch dill, finely chopped

Place eggs in a pot just large enough to hold them and cover with water. Add salt and bring to a boil, reduce to a simmer, and cook for 5 minutes. Test an egg for doneness. Remove eggs and submerge in ice cold water. When cool, peel and reserve.

Heat the olive oil in a saucepan over medium-low heat, add the onion, and cook for 3 to 5 minutes or until the onion becomes very soft. Add the turmeric and pepper flakes and cook for an additional minute. Deglaze with the wine, vinegar, and water; bring to a boil, and add the sugar, salt, and dill. Remove from the heat. When room temperature, pour over the eggs. The eggs are best eaten after a few days but will keep in the refrigerator for up to 3 weeks.

BEET PICKLED EGGS

(SERVES 12)

1 dozen eggs
1 tablespoon salt
3 red beets, peeled
1 cup white wine vinegar
½ cup white wine
½ cup water
1 tablespoon sugar
1 bunch thyme

Place eggs in a pot just large enough to hold them and cover with water. Add salt and bring to a boil, reduce to a simmer, and cook for 5 minutes. Test an egg for doneness. Remove eggs and submerge in ice cold water. When cool, peel eggs and reserve.

Cut the beets into quarters, cover with the vinegar, wine, water, and aromatics, bring to a boil, reduce to a gentle simmer, and cook for 45 minutes or until the beets are tender. Be careful not to reduce the liquid. Remove the beets and save for another day. Pour the pickling liquid over the peeled hard-boiled eggs. The eggs are best eaten after a few days but can keep for up to 3 weeks in the liquid in the refrigerator.

Beaker and Flask

727 SE Washington St
Portland, OR 97214-2219
(503) 235-8180
BeakerandFlask.com
Executive Chef: Ben Bettinger

Beaker and Flask has been the talk of the town for a while. Although its location is not necessarily on everyone's beaten path, the full bar and dining room during each of my visits indicates that location isn't everything. And recently, Rum Club, with snacks that complement the drinks and not vice versa, has joined the Beaker and Flask location. On Tuesdays the parking lot does double duty as an extra kitchen—there is likely to be a whole animal, usually a pig or sometimes a goat, roasting on the giant grill.

The chef, Ben Bettinger, is a genial, adorable creator of interesting, beautiful food that focuses on ingredients, allowing what is on the plate to shine without relying on heavy sauces or fussy preparation.

Originally from Burlington, Vermont, Bettinger made his way out west in 2000, at the tender age of twenty-one, and attended the Western Culinary Institute, which gave him the foundation he felt he lacked after working in kitchens with no formal training. He was offered a job at Paley's Place, one of the premier PDX fine-dining spots, and climbed the ranks during his six-year stay.

At Beaker and Flask, the trout-stuffed deviled eggs are a great flavor pairing. And the pork cheeks served with braised peppers and onions along with tender pickled octopus and aioli make for another remarkable small plate.

The restaurant offers up lots of comfy booths and a few cocktail tables, with a long curved bar that attracts lots of attention. The kitchen is open to the dining room and the big windows make the space feel large and roomy but still personal and friendly. The restaurant does not have the typical Portland feel; rather, it is a bit sleeker and modern. It does, however have the PDX vibe of both professional and personal, and that is one of the things that makes PDX dining so delightful.

Fried Chicken Legs, Beaker and Flask Style

(SERVES 4)

4 8-ounce bone in chicken legs and thighs
1 bunch fresh thyme
Pork fat (enough to cover the legs), available
    at butcher shops and some supermarkets,
    although you might have to ask
Salt and pepper
1 gallon canola oil

For the potato salad:

1½ pounds yellow Yukon potatoes
4 ounces shelled English peas, cooked
    (you can substitute with cooked frozen peas)
1 shallot, brunoise
¼ cup aioli
3 tablespoons sour cream
1 tablespoon chopped fresh dill
1 tablespoon chopped fresh tarragon
1 tablespoon chopped fresh parsley
Salt

For the pickled celery:

1 celery heart (cut into batons)
½ cup white wine vinegar
¼ cup wine
¼ cup water
2 tablespoons salt
2 tablespoons sugar
1 teaspoon chili flakes

For the egg yolk sauce:

4 duck egg yolks (available in gourmet markets)
Salt and pepper
1 teaspoon pink peppercorns

Heat the oven to 325°F.

Season the chicken legs and thighs with salt and pepper and scatter with the thyme. The chicken can be seasoned overnight, or for as short as an hour. Melt the fat and pour over the chicken, cover with parchment paper and foil. Cook the chickens until they're easily pierced with a meat fork or a skewer. This should take about 3 to 4 hours. Let cool in fat. Once cool, remove and rest on a kitchen rack.

Heat the canola oil in a large sided heavy-bottomed pot, until it reaches 350°F, and fry chicken until skin is crisp, 4 to 5 minutes, just to crisp the skin and heat the chicken through. Drain on a paper towel and serve with potato salad, pickled celery, and the egg sauce.

Make the potato salad: Boil potatoes in salted water until easily pierced with a skewer. Cool potatoes, reserve and cut into ½-inch cubes. Mix potatoes with all other ingredients and reserve.

Make the pickled celery: Bring all ingredients to a boil, pour over the celery and leave at room temp until the liquid is at room temperature. Refrigerate and reserve.

Make the egg yolk sauce: Bring a small pot of water to 160°F. Drop in egg yolks and poach for 15 seconds. Lift out of water with a slotted spoon and place in a bowl. Season with salt and black pepper and sauce plate immediately.

Soups

It is no secret that Oregon is not called the Sunshine State, and that's for good reason. Much of the year in Portland, from October through June, it is either raining, about to rain, or just kind of gray and dreary. If you were not born here, it takes some getting used to, and people sometimes become desperate for sun. On the bright side, one good result of the rain is the abundant produce. Soup is the perfect dish because it's a wonderful use of the bounty of fresh vegetables and herbs that people grow in their gardens or pick up at stores or the amazing farmers' markets. In June the soups at Café Nell, for example, are all prepared with the spring harvest.

On a dreary day—and Portland can have a lot of them—soup is the perfect comfort food. It is warming, friendly, and easy. Whether you have it with a great sandwich or enjoy it as a meal by itself—the posole at Autentica, for one—nothing else seems to hit the spot on a cloudy day. Portland restaurants offer a variety of lovely soups, from traditional cheesy onion soup to cold heirloom tomato gazpacho served two ways—one with chervil cream and toasted hazelnuts, the other with roasted tomatoes, garlic spears, and garlicky croutons. Yum.

Café Nell

1987 Northwest Kearney Street
(503) 295-6487
www.CafeNell.com
Chef and Owners: Van and Darren Creely

Café Nell, the small corner restaurant in northwestern Portland, serves very good French/Northwest food—comfort food—in a seventy-seat space that feels homey and relaxed. The place has a neighborhood bistro in Paris vibe, largely because partners Van and Darren Creely go out of their way to make everyone feel welcome and cared for. Both guys are warm and open, making you feel as if you are dining in their home, which is exactly what they have in mind.

Transplanted New Yorkers (Van with a background in marketing and advertising and Darren in cooking) Van and Darren came to Portland to realize their dream of opening a restaurant and to seek a more relaxed lifestyle.

Café Nell is perfect for a romantic dinner for two or for a group of friends wanting a special night out. The dishes reflect the French classics, but Van and Darren extend their repertoire to offer weeknight specials of varying ethnicity at fair prices; Wednesday night's fare of shrimp and grits is a personal favorite. The menu does the most with what is in season, with a minimum of fuss; foods are prepared simply to allow the flavors of the ingredients to shine. The always changing trio of soups offered regularly on the menu is a fun start to the meal. The three soups, which are served together, are different but somehow manage to complement each other, rather than fight tastes that don't pair well. With an emphasis on freshness, simplicity, and seasonality, Café Nell is a delightful spot to spend a long, relaxed evening with friends.

BLACK BEAN SOUP

(SERVES 4–6)

1 tablespoon bacon fat

4 strips bacon cut into ½-inch lardons

½ onion, small dice

1 tablespoon minced garlic

2 cups chicken stock

2 (12-ounce) cans black beans, drained and rinsed

1 tablespoon chopped thyme

1 arbol chile pepper, seeds and stems removed

1 chipotle pepper, seeds and stems removed

Salt and black pepper to taste

1 tablespoon chopped cilantro

Dash of Tabasco

1 teaspoon lime juice

In a medium pot, add the bacon fat and render the bacon on medium heat. Add onions and sauté until translucent. Add garlic and sauté for 2 minutes more.

Add chicken stock, beans, thyme, arbol chile, and chipotle pepper. Bring to a boil and simmer for 20 minutes. Add salt and pepper to taste. Puree in blender in batches with fresh cilantro. Add Tabasco and lime juice to finish.

CHILLED ASPARAGUS SOUP

(SERVES 4–6)

3 tablespoons unsalted butter

2 leeks, rinsed and roughly chopped

2 pounds asparagus, ends trimmed, roughly chopped

4 cups chicken or vegetable stock

Salt and black pepper to taste

1 cup Greek yogurt

Handful of chives, finely chopped

Melt butter in a large saucepan and add leeks. Sauté leeks until they become soft. Add asparagus and stock; bring to a boil. Reduce heat to medium, cover, and let simmer until asparagus is tender.

Carefully ladle stock, leeks, and asparagus and puree in batches using a blender. Transfer puree to a large bowl and season with salt and pepper to taste.

Let mixture cool in refrigerator for at least 3 hours. Serve in a chilled bowl with a dollop of Greek yogurt and garnish with chives.

Vegan Tomato Soup

(SERVES 4–6)

1 tablespoon olive oil
½ yellow onion, small dice
1 carrot, small dice
1 celery stalk, small dice
1 tablespoon minced garlic
½ cup red wine
1 tablespoon chopped thyme
2 (12-ounce) cans diced tomatoes
Salt and black pepper to taste
1 tablespoon lemon juice

In a large pot sauté the onion, carrot and celery in the olive oil for 10 to 12 minutes. Add garlic and sauté 2 minutes more. Add red wine and thyme.

Simmer and reduce by half. Add tomatoes, bring to a boil, and simmer 30 minutes. Add salt and pepper to taste. Puree until smooth. Add lemon juice to finish.

BRASSERIE MONTMARTRE

626 SOUTHWEST PARK AVENUE
(503) 236-3036
WWW.BRASSERIEPORTLAND.COM
EXECUTIVE CHEF AND OWNER: PASCAL CHUREAU
CHEF: MICHAEL HANAGHAN

A number of French restaurants have opened in Portland in the past year. There was word around town that this city was too small to support them. And because PDX is so Northwest-centric, there was further grist for the "it will never make it" rumor mill.

As for me, I had faith. French food is wonderful. It is different than the Northwest food culture, but in some vital ways, it is also the same. There is an emphasis on seasonality, winter dishes and summer dishes, never putting an unripe tomato on anything, and totally digging making and eating charcuterie, cheese, bread, and wine. Sounds familiar? Oui!

Brasserie Montmartre is situated in downtown Portland, near Little Bird (see page 121) restaurant, and gets a busy lunch crowd. At noon, the restaurant already starts to fill up. It draws a different crowd—businesspeople, shoppers, and theater goers, mostly—and there is still the occasional east side hipster. It has gone through lots of personnel and menu changes and recently reopened with a whole new crew, and with fabulous results.

The onion soup is perfection, a rich and deeply flavored stock, two melted cheeses, and a toasted brioche slice. The mixed salad at its side, with the addition of crumbled Roquefort (a luxury these days due to the huge import tariff on that pillar of cheese) is like getting together with an old special food friend. Bruce had a crepe with pork belly and arugula, and I had the duck confit on a bed of roasted onions and potatoes that was one of the best things I have eaten in a long time, and I am constantly eating amazing food.

However, the pièce de résistance is the fries. We had two of the five offered, the duck fat fries and the truffle fries, and I must admit I wanted to order the other choices as well: pommes frites, pork belly, and the foie gras/Szechuan pepper fries. Bruce, who experienced the dream of living in Paris for five years and eating well, said he thought they might be the best fries he had ever had. And they are the perfect fry. With ketchup and aioli. Bliss.

The dessert menu is beyond tempting. Very soon I will be back for the malted milk chocolate mousse, the lavender peach crisp, and the lemon thyme fritters.

And the fries.

Soupe à l'Oignon

French Onion Soup

(SERVES 6–8)

2 quarts rich beef stock

¼ pound unsalted butter

½ cup water

5 pounds yellow onions, julienned, no core

1 tablespoon all-purpose flour

Kosher salt

Per serving:

10 ounces onion soup base

1 brioche crouton, thin slice, toasted

3 slices Swiss Emmentaler

¼ cup grated Comté cheese

Bring the beef stock to a boil, skim, and reduce to a simmer for about 1 to 2 hours. Simmering the stock creates more body and intensifies the flavor.

Make a beurre monté by melting the butter with the water in a large saucepan. Add the julienned onions and cook slowly until caramelized and reduced to about 2 cups. Dust the caramelized onions with the flour. Add the salt and the stock.

Simmer 45 to 60 minutes. Skim frequently.

The onions should cook very slowly until they reach a dark caramel color. When they are finished, adjust the seasoning and cool.

To serve, heat soup and season. Add to bowl and top with the brioche crouton. Top with the sliced cheese first, then the grated cheese.

Gratinée under the broiler until the cheese is melted and has good color.

IT'S ALL IN THE DETAILS

The more basic the soup, the more critical the details: Slice the onion uniformly; brown them very slowly and evenly; slice the bread ½-inch thick, drying it completely in the oven; and serve the soup in an appropriately sized bowl. There's a lot going on in a simple recipe like onion soup, and when you hit it right, there's nothing more satisfying than either cooking it or eating it.

ELEPHANTS

MULTIPLE LOCATIONS
WWW.ELEPHANTSDELI.COM
HEAD CHEF: SCOTT WALKER
OWNER: ANNE WEAVER

When I first moved to Portland, I lived within a couple of miles of Elephants and got there often. (At that time there was only one; now there are five.) Elephants calls itself a delicatessen, but that is an understatement. The only thing "deli" about it is that there's meat. The huge store is European in feel, selling both food items and things for the home

that are sophisticated and unusual. I go there to buy friends cool gifts, both edible and not. It's the kind of stuff you don't see everywhere: beautiful glassware, interesting plates and candles, unusual oils and delicacies. I always want to buy something.

But certainly it is the food that draws the crowds. The Elephants locations have a ton of choices, a small display area with some trattoria-inspired foods, and then all the prepared foods that you can buy by the portion or the pound. The 22nd Street store is by far the largest, with the greatest selection of foods and interesting gift ideas for the kitchen and home. They make good pizza, very good calamari, ditto for the fish and chips. But one must not miss the soups. I know a bunch of people who, if they find they may be getting a little sniffle, will get over to Elephants to get a pint or quart of soup to go. All the soups are good, but from my first taste of Mama Leone's, I felt it needed to be shared—it is my favorite soup in the world. It is delicious, chunky yet velvety, with a tomato flavor that is mellowed by the cream, and is, next to chicken soup, the world's best comfort food.

Desserts are good, too, with several excellent cookies and very tasty cupcakes that are hard to pass up. On my last visit I had the absolutely yummy chicken enchiladas verdes, perfectly tender chicken breasts layered with cream cheese, cheddar, corn tortillas, and a zesty tomatillo sauce, and served with a homemade salsa. Having a bit of room left, I got a triple chocolate cookie for the road. This is no deli.

Mama Leone's Soup

(SERVES 6–8)

½ pound boneless chicken breast
Salt and black pepper to taste
1 onion, diced
3 ribs celery, diced
2 tablespoons canola oil
3 tablespoons salted butter
1 tablespoon minced garlic
½ teaspoon tarragon
½ teaspoon thyme
1 teaspoon oregano
2 teaspoons paprika
2 teaspoons kosher salt
½ teaspoon freshly ground black pepper
10 tablespoons all-purpose flour
½ gallon fresh chicken stock
12 ounces canned tomatoes, diced
¾ cup cream
2 cups chopped spinach

Preheat oven to 350°F. Place chicken on a sheet pan, season with salt and pepper, and bake for 15 to 20 minutes. When cool enough to handle, dice the chicken and reserve.

In a large heavy pot, sauté onions and celery in oil and butter until onions are translucent. Add garlic, tarragon, thyme, oregano, paprika, salt, and pepper. Cook, stirring for 5 minutes.

Add flour and stir. Add chicken stock and bring to a boil. Add tomatoes, reserved chicken, and cream; simmer for 20 to 30 minutes.

Just before serving, add the spinach.

23 Hoyt: A New American Tavern

529 Northwest 23rd Avenue
(503) 445-7400
www.23hoyt.com
Executive Chef: Amber Webster
Owner: Bruce Carey

This gentrified PDX neighborhood is host to a number of spots that serve good food and alcohol. 23 Hoyt is a large, two-story restaurant that reflects the feeling of this upscale part of town. Although 23 Hoyt will accommodate up to 160 people (including the outside tables), the place is set up to feel like a series of rooms so there are spots that are intimate and cozy. The room displays a Northwest eclectic mix of grays and greens, art, antlers and flowers, and full-size trees in giant planters. The bar seats ten, and there is an excellent selection of top-shelf libations.

Chef Amber Webster, born in Whitefish, Montana, began working in kitchens at just sixteen. She moved to San Francisco to attend the California Culinary Academy, a

Cordon Bleu program, to get a strong cooking foundation, adding to her already somewhat polished skills. Webster did some catering there while attending school and shortly thereafter moved to San Diego, where she worked at the Marine Room on the beach in La Jolla. After several years, a cooking partner offered her the sous chef position at 23 Hoyt, and in December 2011 she was promoted to head chef. With a love of cooking and the thrill of the weekend dinner and brunch rush, Webster has a following eager to enjoy her house-made pizzettes topped with the freshest offerings of the season. It is not unusual on a Saturday night to sell sixty or more of this crispy, often cheesy treat. Beer-braised beef cheeks, with preserved lemon polenta, is magical, as is the pan-roasted salmon with flavors of sweet caramelized fennel and charred onions.

23 Hoyt has one of the best happy hours in town, and it's a great way to try some of the items on the regular menu at a fraction of the cost. Before you leave, have a couple of Webster's salted chocolate chip cookies—they are out of this world.

Carrot Soup with Chervil Cream

(SERVES 6)

For the soup:

⅓ cup unsalted butter, cut into pieces
1 medium onion, medium dice
3 cloves garlic, roughly chopped
2 medium leeks, rinsed, greens removed, medium dice
2 tablespoons salt
1 quart plus 2 tablespoons vegetable or chicken stock
1 pound carrots, peeled, medium dice
½ cup carrot juice
½ cup orange juice

For the cream:

½ cup heavy whipping cream
2 tablespoons fresh chervil, chopped
Pinch of salt
Chervil leaves for garnish

Melt butter in a saucepan. Add onion, garlic, leeks, and salt and 2 tablespoons stock; sweat over medium heat until translucent, aromatic, and very soft. Add 1 quart stock, increase heat to high, and bring to a hard boil. Add carrots and keep on high heat. Cook carrots as quickly as possible over high heat until just soft enough to puree, then remove from heat. (Cooking the carrots quickly on high heat will retain the bright color and flavor that is desired for this soup.) Just before blending, add the carrot and orange juices. Puree in a blender until silky smooth.

Prepare the cream: In a medium mixing bowl whip the heavy cream until thick and foamy (the cream should resemble pancake batter). Fold in chopped chervil and season with salt.

To serve: Ladle the hot soup into serving bowls, then spoon in a dollop of semi-whipped chervil cream into the center of each bowl. Garnish with whole chervil leaves.

Mother's Bistro & Bar

212 Southwest Stark Street
(503) 464-1122
WWW.MOTHERSBISTRO.COM
CHEF AND OWNER: LISA SCHROEDER

Mother's is one of the only themed restaurants in Portland. As themed restaurants go, this one is very sweet, and the food is very good. The focus is on the meals mothers cook for their families all over the world. Chef and owner Lisa Schroeder still has her native New York persona; she is bold, honest, warm, fun, and full of nonstop energy. She still works the line at the restaurant, wanting it all to be just right.

The rooms are motherly, with warm fabrics, soft happy colors, comfy chairs, and an eclectic mix of yellow and green wainscoting, tieback sheer curtains, and crystal chandeliers. As a finishing touch, the walls are covered with artwork that depicts motherhood. As if that's not enough, Mother's runs a mother-of-the-month program, featuring a photograph and bio of a mom from a faraway country who's cooked a special dish for her children.

Mother's gets a huge breakfast/brunch crowd, and there is almost always a wait. But once you are seated and the food comes, it is all forgotten. Crunchy french toast dipped in cornflakes and browned in butter is killer, as is the stuffed frittata, an open-faced omelet with bacon, Cheddar cheese, and potatoes, topped with sour cream and green onions.

Lunches are great, particularly the pierogi (handmade potato dumplings with fried onions and sour cream) and the Caesar salad. At dinnertime, it doesn't hurt to start off with a bowl of Schroeder's matzo ball soup or the oniony and tasty chopped chicken liver. I never skip the chicken with dumplings, and my husband, Bruce, goes for the meat loaf or pot roast almost every time. Every dessert is a winner, a personal favorite being the deep and sinfully rich devil's food cake. This is the ultimate comfort food restaurant, and you leave feeling satisfied and bathed in your own mother's culinary love.

BELLE'S MATZO BALL SOUP

(SERVES 8–10)

For the chicken soup:

2 whole chickens and other carcasses, if available
2 yellow onions, peeled and left whole
4 stalks celery, peeled and left whole
4 carrots, peeled and left whole
4 parsnips, peeled and left whole
1 bunch Italian parsley, stems and all
Fresh cold water to cover
Salt and freshly ground black pepper to taste
2 cups finely diced carrot
2 cups finely diced celery
1 bunch chopped fresh dill (for garnish)

For the matzo balls:

¼ cup melted chicken fat or vegetable oil
4 eggs, slightly beaten
1 cup matzo meal (available in the kosher section
   of the supermarket)
2 teaspoons salt
2 tablespoons cold chicken soup
2 tablespoons soda water (club soda)

Start the chicken soup: In a big pot just large enough to hold the chickens, put in the chickens and vegetables (up to the diced vegetables). Add only enough cold water to cover the chickens (about 1½ gallons). Bring to a boil and skim any scum that rises to the surface and discard. Season soup lightly with salt and pepper.

Simmer the broth, uncovered, for at least 3 hours. Lift the chicken from the pot and set aside until cool enough to handle. Strain the rest of the broth into a clean pot.

Add the diced carrots and celery to the strained broth, bring to a boil, and cook until just tender.

While the vegetables are cooking, pick through the chicken, trying to leave the pieces as large as possible, discarding the bones. Set aside.

Prepare the matzo balls: In a large mixing bowl, whisk together the chicken fat, eggs, matzo meal, and salt. Add the soup and soda water and mix well.

Cover mixture and place bowl in the refrigerator for about 15 minutes.

Place 1 gallon of water and 1 tablespoon of salt in a large pot and bring to a boil.

Remove matzo ball mixture from refrigerator, and using an ice cream dipper (this ensures that the matzo balls are uniform in size) scoop out equal amounts (about 1 inch in diameter) onto a cookie sheet. With wet hands, roll each scoopful of the matzo mixture so that it is shaped like a ball and drop the balls into the boiling water.

Reduce the heat so the water is at a simmer, cover the pot, and cook matzo balls about 30 minutes.

Lift the matzo balls out with a slotted spoon and place in serving bowls.

To serve: Add some of the cooked, picked chicken back to the soup pot (you can make chicken salad with the rest of the boiled chicken); taste soup for seasoning, adjusting with salt and freshly ground pepper, as needed.

Ladle broth, chicken, and vegetables into bowls with the matzo balls, sprinkle with fresh chopped dill, and serve.

Notes: You can omit the matzo balls and serve the chicken soup with noodles instead. Cook the noodles separately according to package directions and strain, keeping them separate until ready to serve. Place them in serving bowls and ladle soup on top.

If making the matzo balls ahead of time, keep them in the cooking liquid until ready to serve, then lift them out with a slotted spoon and place in serving bowls. This will prevent the balls from drying out.

COME TO . . .
POSSESS SOME O . . .
BEAUTIFUL COLORS . . .
FLAVORS IN THE WORLD.

House Made

SPANISH BLEN

STUDDED WITH RIPE
AND GREEN OLIVES
PERFUMED WITH THE
OF THE SPANIS
COUNTRYSIDE

ANCHOVY
STUFFED

SPANISH ANCHOVIES STUFFED
INSIDE CALIFORNIA
SEVILLANO OLIVES. DOES IT
GET ANY BETTER?

Yakuza Lounge

5411 Northeast 30th Avenue
(503) 450-0893
www.yakuzalounge.com
Owner: Dayna McErlean
Chef: David Gaspar de Alba

Yakuza is an extraordinarily beautiful restaurant. During my visit on a beautiful Portland summer day, I was amazed at how lovely it is. The dining room and bar area are Japanese inspired: elegant and understated. Local artist Andrew Rossi worked with the owner, Dayna McErlean, to create hand-painted walls featuring a beautiful cherry blossom tree and some open parasols, along with custom-made tables and benches. It is an entrancing setting. We walked though the dining room, past the chef's table that can seat up to twelve, and into the perfect Japanese garden, with a wooden bridge, running water, and a soaking tub. Come on, this is so amazing. It's one of the little magical places around Portland where things get so green and smell so good, and you sit out back and wish you could stay forever.

The chef, David Gaspar de Alba, has a light hand, and everything tastes pure, simple, yet dramatic. The izakaya-style food is a great balance of tastes and textures, always

fresh and always beautiful. The menu changes with the daily deliveries. Some favorites: The cheese-stuffed squash blossoms, battered and fried, are light and a brilliant rendition of that classic dish, and scallop tempura with shredded phyllo and creamy, spicy sauce is delicate and unusual. Along with the upscale small bites, you can order perhaps the best burger in Portland, so this place is perfect after all. Come for the decor and the menu, but don't forget to sample the amazing cocktails and desserts. The sugar snap pea martini—yes, you read that correctly—is surprisingly tasty, and desserts are a great excuse to stick around.

ASARI MISO SOUP

(SERVES 2)

12 fresh Manila clams
2 cups dashi stock*
1 ounce soft tofu (¼ inch dice)
1 teaspoon wakame seaweed (soaked)
1½ tablespoon red miso
2 teaspoons scallion, finely sliced
Dash sansho pepper

For the dashi stock: (Makes 2 cups)*

1 (5 x 3-inch) piece of kombu
4 cups filtered water
1¼ ounces bonito flakes

Dashi stock is made from kombu, a type of sea kelp, and bonito flakes.

In a steel pot, simply place a postcard size piece of kombu along with 4 cups of filtered water. Let sit for 20 minutes, then turn the heat on. As soon as the water comes to a boil, remove dashi and add 1¼ ounces bonito flakes. Let this sit for 30 more minutes then strain through a fine sieve. Freeze-dried granules called dashi-no-moto can be used to make a quick dashi, but at the restaurant it is made from scratch.

Before you start, place ½ teaspoon of wakame seaweed in a quart of room temperature water, let soak for 10 minutes, then strain.

To make your miso soup grab a pot with a tight fitting lid, place 12 Manila clams and 2 cups dashi, cover and bring to boil. Once clams have opened turn off heat and carefully place clams in bowls, discarding any that did not open.

To the bowls add your diced tofu and wakame. To the remaining dashi whisk in miso until well incorporated, adding more miso if you like a bolder flavor. Once miso is in the dashi stock do not boil.

Carefully pour your miso into ready bowls and garnish with fresh cut scallions and a dash of Japanese sansho pepper.

AUTENTICA

5507 NORTHEAST 3OTH AVENUE
(503) 287-7555
WWW.AUTENTICAPORTLAND.COM
CHEF AND OWNER: OSWALDO BIBIANO

Dining at Autentica is like eating at a friend's house. Everyone is warm and welcoming, and the room, while not small, still manages to be cozy. Sitting in the back garden, which is brightly colored and filled with flowers, you feel as if you have been transported to another place entirely.

Oswaldo Bibiano came to Portland in his early twenties after working, from the age of fourteen, in the kitchens in Acapulco, several hours from his hometown of Guerrero. He knew early on that cooking was his passion, and he developed from his grandmother and mother, both wonderful home cooks, an appreciation for all the time and patience that go into preparing authentic Mexican food.

The menu is not typical Mexican fare. Autentica does offer a plate that includes two different enchiladas and a chile relleno, but each is prepared so artfully as to give diners the feeling that they are finally experiencing these foods the way they were meant to be. The *queso fundido con chorizo* (Oaxacan melting cheese and chorizo served with fresh tortillas) is beyond magnificent, and the *tacos al pastor* is without question the best I have ever eaten. The thirty-spice chicken mole is complex and sheer perfection, and the *camarones al autentico mojo de ajo* (deep-sea Mexican prawns cooked with garlic sauce) could not be any better.

Every Thursday night, as it was in Guerrero, is posole night at Autentica. Posole, a thick soup made in just about every household in Bibiano's hometown, is a traditional dish originally from the Pacific coast region of Jalisco and is usually made with pork, hominy (dried maize kernels), garlic, onion, chile peppers, cilantro, and broth. The combination of flavors in both the soup and the garnishes makes every bite a wonderful, unique surprise.

People from all over Portland have made posole night a tradition, and the giant soup pot is empty before the restaurant closes for the night. At Autentica, everything is made from scratch. With the original being a bit too ambitious for the home cook, Chef Bibiano has given a recipe for his wonderful soup that you can make at home without having to quit your day job.

POSOLE

(SERVES 8–10)

2 pounds pork leg with bone, or pork butt

12 cloves whole garlic

Half of an onion, either yellow or white, sliced in half to make 2 quarters

2 tablespoons salt

3 pounds dried clean, soaked corn hominy, or 2 medium (15-ounce) cans of any store-bought hominy, drained

3 tablespoons oregano

For garnish:

Shredded cabbage

Crumbled queso fresco (fresh Mexican cheese)

Diced Serrano peppers

Diced white onions

Diced radishes

Diced avocado

Lime wedges

Tortilla chips

In a large pot with 5 gallons of water, add the pork, 9 garlic cloves, 1 quarter of the onion, and salt. Boil the meat for 1 hour. (Add more water if necessary.)

Add the corn hominy and the 2 tablespoons of the oregano to the soup. Lower the heat to low and let the soup slowly reduce to a 2-gallon portion, or until the hominy and meat are tender. (Do not let the hominy break down.) The hominy kernel should be whole and tender.

In a blender add 1 cup of the hominy, 2 cups broth, half a quarter of onion, 3 cloves of garlic, and 1 more tablespoon oregano. (Blend until it reaches a liquid but still somewhat chunky concoction.) Add the mixture to the soup, and simmer over a low flame for 10 to 15 minutes (be sure to stir well throughout).

To serve: Ladle soup into bowls. For garnish, add shredded cabbage, crumbled queso fresco, diced Serrano peppers and onions, diced radishes, and diced avocado. Stir the condiments well and squeeze a lime wedge. Don't forget the chips.

Brunch

Portlanders love breakfast and brunch. There are places solely dedicated to those two meals, and most of the best restaurants in town serve brunch at least one day on the weekend. For me, brunch has always been a special occasion meal, when a friend was visiting from out of town or there was something to celebrate. Because it is a meal I have just begun to appreciate, I am still on the fence about which way to go—breakfast or lunch—because you do need to make that decision.

For people in Portland, breakfast and brunch are part of their regular routines, not just for those special times, and the expectations of great food are as high as they are for dinner.

There is no question that this meal is taken seriously by the chefs of Portland, resulting in dishes such as fried chicken and spoon bread from Country Cat, the hash from Broder, and the migas with a few dashes of hot sauce from Bakery Bar. If it is not a big meal you want, there are wonderful treats like the Manchego, mushroom, and cheese biscuit from Crema Bakery (see page 158), or the perfect Irish soda bread scones from Grand Central Bakery (see page 176). And if you want a very different morning dining experience, you can head out to 82nd Street and have phenomenal dim sum, or to Andy Ricker's favorite Ha & VI, a Vietnamese noodle place that is extraordinary and often runs out of the house-made noodles by noon.

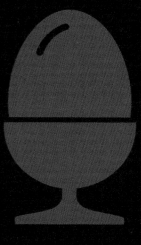

Toast

5222 Southeast 52nd Avenue
(503) 774-1020
www.toastpdx.com
Chef: A Toast collaboration, too many to mention
Owner: Donald Kotler

Hundreds of drawings, by both kids and adults, adorn the walls of this thirty-five-seat restaurant on the edge of the Woodstock neighborhood. Tiny antique toasters line a few shelves, and there is a blackboard with the daily specials. The place is hopping with local families, Reedies (the super-smart people who attend nearby Reed College), and others coming from all over town for the glorious breakfast and lunch offerings. (Dinner is also served three nights a week.)

We arrived for breakfast around 11:00 a.m. and got the last blue plate daily special: white beans with kale, collards, and chard, with a poached egg and a Padrón pepper coulis. (Padróns are not around for all that long, so I hate to pass them up.) Tiny and terrific scones are brought to the table as soon as you are seated, whetting your appetite

for more. The house-made granola, called Hippies Use Front Door, is outstanding, and the curried tofu scramble is a favorite with vegetarians as well as meat eaters.

Sandwiches are delish, and only the freshest ingredients are used. Farmers drop by throughout the day to deliver just about everything the restaurant serves. No big supply houses, just small farms, make things as local as possible. On my last visit, gorgeous heirloom tomatoes were being admired by the chef and cooks, right off the back of the farmer's truck.

Desserts are also outstanding, and sitting at the counter we got to watch former cook Michael Johnston prepare his grandma Martha Johnston's recipe for huckleberry and raspberry pie, which by all accounts is beyond belief perfection.

Drinks are creative and fun, both nonalcoholic and the hard stuff. The blood orange mimosa is a refreshing and potent libation, and the Morning Glory, a blend of black currant, lemonade, ginger syrup, and tequila, is almost too easy to drink.

Dinners are very reasonably priced, and the lamb shank and the gnocchi are outstanding. This is a terrific place to get a well-priced and well-made meal, for breakfast, lunch, or dinner. And it's a popular spot for people on their bicycles; on my last visit there were at least ten bikes out front, and half of the people in the restaurant were in riding clothes. It's so Portland.

"Go Home Thomas"
Egg and Sausage Sandwiches

(SERVES 6)

For the muffins: (Makes 12 average-size English muffins—freeze half for later use)

3¼ plus 1 cups all-purpose flour

3¼ cups bread flour

1 tablespoon plus 1 teaspoon salt

1 tablespoon plus 1 teaspoon dry active yeast

1 tablespoon sugar

3 cups cold water

1 cup cornmeal

Special equipment: **Griddle**

In a medium bowl mix the dry ingredients (not including cornmeal). Add the water and mix until all ingredients are incorporated. Place in a large bowl and cover; let the dough double in size (2 to 3 hours at room temperature, or in the refrigerator overnight).

After the dough has doubled, using equal parts cornmeal and flour mixture, liberally flour a flat surface and roll out the dough until approximately ¾- to 1-inch thick.

Cut molds and place on a well-oiled griddle on low to medium heat.

Let brown on one side, flip, and oil again.

The muffins will be done when they push back readily in the center.

For the sausage:

1 pound ground pork

2 cloves garlic, minced

½ teaspoon thyme

Smoked paprika to taste

Salt and black pepper to taste

1 cup white grated cheddar (for garnish)

In a medium bowl combine the sausage ingredients. Let sit in refrigerator for 12 to 24 hours. Divide into six portions and press into circles. Cook on griddle for 5 to 6 minutes per side. Drain on paper towels.

For the eggs:

12 large eggs

Salt and black pepper to taste

2 tablespoons unsalted butter

In a medium bowl whisk the eggs with salt and pepper. Add butter to a nonstick pan and stir to cook. Keep stirring the eggs into the center of the pan; try to keep the eggs almost omeletlike, not small pieces.

To serve: Toast six muffins until golden brown. Place a sausage patty on six halves, then some scrambled eggs, top with cheese, and cover with other muffin halves.

COFFEE

Portland ranks 5th nationally in number of coffee shops per capita. Not bad. Maybe it's because of the rain; people either need that pick-me-up on a long, grey day or a great mocha latte to take the damp and chill out of your tattoos. There are so many great places to stop, have a chewy cookie, and a serious cup of Joe. And coffee is serious business here in the Pacific Northwest—it is not hard to get a good cup. Baristas are highly respected, like the chef or bartender, and if so inclined you can talk about coffee for hours. I was not a coffee drinker before moving to Portland. Now, it's not so much that I need it to get me started, but rather that I just love the way it tastes. Hot or cold, light or dark, topped with foam or a sprinkling of cocoa, I am now one of the many in PDX proud of the quality of our beans.

NEL CENTRO

1408 SOUTHWEST 6TH AVENUE
(503) 484-1099
WWW.NELCENTRO.COM
CHEF D'ENTREPRISE AND OWNER: DAVID MACHADO
CHEF DE CUISINE: MATTHEW BEMIS

Located in the Hotel Modera, a hip boutique hotel in downtown Portland, Chef David Machado's most recent venture, Nel Centro, is warm and light-filled. Hotel restaurants fall into a different category, and sometimes reviewing them is like comparing apples and oranges, but I could not leave David Machado out of a book about the Portland food scene. Machado's career in PDX started in 1991, when he opened Pazzo, a well-loved Italian restaurant in downtown Portland. From there he went on to open two of his own places: Lauro Kitchen and the Indian restaurant Vindahlo, before opening Nel Centro in 2009.

The cuisine of Nel Centro is rooted in the Italian and French Riviera. As a fan of some of those regions' specialties, I was overjoyed to find salt cod croquettes and an incredibly rich and tender daube of beef. Ravioli niçoise, faithful to the region, is authentic and inspiring. Desserts are outstanding, with personal favorites being the blackberry bread pudding with salt-studded caramel ice cream and the lemon pistachio cake with blueberry compote. Here, this time, the Riviera joins company, once again, with the Northwest.

Because it is in a hotel, there is great detail given to both breakfast and brunch. The brioche breakfast sandwich with scrambled eggs, pork loin, Fontina, and an herbed aioli is a splendid way to start the day, complete with good coffee. Another stand-out item is the eggs with griddled polenta and sage hollandaise. It was my first experience combining that earthy spice and creamy sauce, and it is a wonderful way to go.

SANGRIA

A wonderful recipe that I've been making for years. (SERVES 10–12)

2 bottles red Spanish table wine
2 cups orange juice
1 cup pomegranate juice
1 cup brandy
½ cup triple sec
⅔ cup simple syrup, or more to taste
    (equal parts sugar and water, heated
    until sugar dissolves, cooled)

1 lime, peeled and sectioned
1 orange, peeled and sectioned
1 cup sliced strawberries
1 cup gently crushed blackberries

Mix all ingredients together and let stand in a container or pitcher for at least 24 hours in the refrigerator before serving.

Eggs with Griddled Polenta and Sage Hollandaise

(SERVES 4)

For the polenta:

4 cups chicken stock
1 cup polenta
¾ cup unsalted butter
½ cup heavy cream
½ cup grated Parmesan
Pinch of nutmeg
Salt and black pepper to taste

For the hollandaise:

1 cup white wine
1 tablespoon white wine vinegar
3 peppercorns
2 bay leaves
4 large egg yolks
2 cups clarified butter
1 teaspoon lemon juice
2 dashes of Tabasco
Salt and black pepper to taste
2 tablespoons chopped fresh sage
2 tablespoons unsalted butter
4 large poached eggs

Prepare the polenta: In a medium saucepan, boil chicken stock. Whisk in polenta. Cook, stirring constantly, 30 to 40 minutes. When polenta has thickened and is all the way cooked, add butter, heavy cream, Parmesan, nutmeg, salt, and pepper. Pour onto baking sheet and let cool until set. Cut squares or circles and sear to order.

Prepare the sage hollandaise: Reduce white wine and white wine vinegar, peppercorns, and bay leaves.

Cool and add the egg yolks. Over a double boiler whisk the eggs so they fluff up and become creamy; be sure not to scramble.

Slowly add the clarified butter while whisking. Once all the butter is incorporated, add the lemon juice, Tabasco, salt, and pepper. Add the chopped sage and mix well.

To serve: Cut four pieces of polenta. Melt the butter in a skillet and allow to foam. Add the polenta and cook until golden on both sides. Place the polenta on four plates. Place a poached egg on each polenta square or round and top with the sage hollandaise.

Fat City Café

7820 Southwest Capitol Highway
(503) 245-5457
www.fatcitycafe.net
Owners: Helen and Mark Johnson
Chef: Jose Ramirez

In a city filled with many distinctly different neighborhoods, there is one part of town that feels like no other: Multnomah Village is very much like a village within a city. One of the features that set it apart is that you really can't see anything else when you are there—no tall buildings, no bridges, very little traffic. It is small and charming with a collection of shops that seem to cater to a specific clientele. Multnomah Village feels artsy, perhaps

like a town on Martha's Vineyard; it has the feeling that not much has changed over the years, nor has it gone through the gentrification that has affected many PDX communities.

At the heart of this quaint village is Fat City Cafe, one of the few true diners in Portland. It has a bit of a colorful past, including the 1987 firing of Police Chief Jim Davis by then mayor of Portland Bud Clark. As the famous story goes, Portland's mayor met his police chief at the restaurant. Over coffee, the mayor fired the police chief, saying simply: "Read my lips. You're fired." Today's customers can sit in the same booth with the article and a sign over their table that reads: "The police chief was fired here." Cute as this story is, I go for the great food, not to sit at that table.

The walls are covered with at least one hundred old license plates, and the old-fashioned paper placemats and knickknacks from the cafe's steady and loyal clientele reflect the businesses and history of the neighborhood.

The portions at this off-the-beaten-path cafe are large, with many items worth ordering. It is one of those places where we always seem to order something "for the table," which is code or justification for an extra entree.

Simple pancakes are perfect, the Frisbee-size freshly baked cinnamon rolls are divine, and the skillet and scrambled egg dishes are all first rate. The staff is friendly, the food comes out quickly, and the coffee is good and constantly being topped off.

After eating, walk off your meal and stroll through the cafe's neighborhood to explore the great shops, including a lovely bookstore, a bead shop, and an interesting Middle Eastern shop that sells great soaps and towels. Also, check out John's Market, with its superb beer selection. Before getting in your car, you might want to run back into Fat City and get a giant cinnamon roll for the road.

Fat City Sizzle

(SERVES 1)

3 tablespoons canola oil
¼ cup diced onion
¼ cup diced green pepper
1 large baking potato, cooked, peeled,
    and shredded
3 tablespoons shredded cheddar
2 medium-size eggs
Salt and black pepper to taste

Heat the canola oil in a large nonstick skillet or on a griddle. Sauté the onion and pepper until soft, 7 to 9 minutes. Add the shredded potato, turn up heat, and cook for 4 to 5 minutes until golden brown on top.

Flip the potato mixture over and cook for an additional 4 to 5 minutes.

In a small sauté pan cook the eggs on both sides until medium doneness.

Place the hash browns on a large plate. Sprinkle with the shredded cheese, and top with the eggs. Season with salt and pepper.

Cinnamon Roll French Toast

(SERVES 1)

2 large eggs, lightly beaten
½ cup milk
1 teaspoon vanilla
1 cinnamon roll, sliced in rounds
2 tablespoons unsalted butter
Butter and maple syrup

In a large shallow dish combine the eggs, milk, and vanilla and whisk. Add the cinnamon roll slices and allow to sit in the milk mixture, turning once.

In a large saucepan melt the 2 tablespoons butter over medium heat. Add the cinnamon rolls, drain off liquid, and cook for 2 to 3 minutes per side. They should be light golden brown.

Serve with butter and maple syrup.

PINE STATE BISCUITS

3640 SOUTHEAST BELMONT STREET
(503) 236-3346
2204 NORTHEAST ALBERTA STREET
(503) 477-6605
WWW.PINESTATEBISCUITS.COM
EXECUTIVE CHEFS AND OWNERS: WALT ALEXANDER, KEVIN ATCHLEY, AND BRIAN SNYDER

There are a couple of Pine State Biscuit diner-style restaurants in Portland, both on the east side of the river. No surprise, they are very casual and funky. You go to the counter to place your order and ogle every plate that goes by while you wait. Sometimes there can be a long line, and sometimes you get lucky and sit right down. There are three guys behind the shops, which started out as a stand at a farmers' market, which is not unusual here. After achieving success, Walt Alexander, Kevin Atchley, and Brian Snyder opened up a small biscuit shop on Belmont Street, where folks can enjoy a wholesome (well, maybe not the perfect word) breakfast or lunch seven days a week, rain or shine.

Esquire magazine in 2008 chose Pine State Biscuit's Reggie Deluxe as one of the best sandwiches in the entire nation. It is a great breakfast, and when you eat one with their spectacular home fries, you are set for the day.

The restaurant on Belmont is very small, whereas the Alberta location is bigger and has outside covered seating. The guys have kept it simple, with a blackboard menu that has about a dozen choices. If you are a biscuit purist, you can order a biscuit with jam, butter and honey, fruit and whipped cream, or a house-made pimento spread, which is one of the best I've had in PDX. The Stumptown coffee is always good, and when you waddle out you may think you will never eat again.

THE REGGIE DELUXE

(SERVES 4)

For the buttermilk fried chicken:

1 quart buttermilk (approximately)
Cayenne pepper to taste
4 (5-ounce) chicken breasts
3 large eggs
Hot sauce (optional)
1 cup self-rising flour
½ teaspoon black pepper (approximately)
Seasoning for chicken (garlic powder, onion powder, and cayenne)

For the savory sausage gravy:

1 tablespoon vegetable oil
1 large onion, minced
1 pound breakfast sausage
1 stick unsalted butter
1 cup flour (approximately)
¼ cup heavy cream (room temperature)
½ cup water (approximately)
1 pint whole milk (room temperature)
1 tablespoon sea salt (approximately)
Seasoning to taste (salt, pepper, and cayenne)

Oil for frying (peanut is best, but canola or soybean
   will work)
4 biscuits
12 strips bacon, cooked and drained on paper towels
4 large eggs, fried over easy
Shredded cheddar cheese (for garnish)

Prepare the chicken: Marinate chicken 24 to 48
hours before you're ready to fry. To marinate:
Pour buttermilk into container with secure lid.
Generously sprinkle cayenne over buttermilk and
mix thoroughly with whisk. Slice chicken breasts
in half, running your knife parallel to the cutting
board so you have two thin pieces each. Add
chicken to the buttermilk mixture. Secure the lid
and place the container in the refrigerator.

One hour before cooking, in a medium-size bowl
beat eggs (adding a splash of water). Add hot
sauce to the egg mixture if desired. In a large
bowl, combine flour and pepper. Drain chicken
in colander and lay breasts flat on baking sheet.
Season chicken with something delicious, like
Cajun spice or your own secret blend. Dip the
seasoned chicken in the egg, then dredge in the
flour mixture. Place prepared chicken on a clean
sheet pan and store in the refrigerator until ready
to cook. It's best to allow some time for the egg-
flour coating to become doughy before you fry.

Prepare the gravy: Place oil in a large saucepan
over medium heat, add the onion, and cook until
opaque. Mix in sausage and cook mixture until
the sausage is browned but not fully cooked.
Reduce heat to low. If desired, drain excess
grease at this point.

While the sausage is cooking, begin melting
the butter over medium-low heat in a separate
saucepan. Once melted completely, begin
adding flour slowly, stirring constantly until a
smooth, thick, light colored roux develops,
approximately 10 to 15 minutes. Stir in a dash
of heavy cream if roux becomes too thick or
clumpy.

Crank the sausage mixture up to medium-
high heat and add just enough water to make
the mixture soupy (approximately ½ cup),
and continue to cook over medium-high heat,
stirring frequently for 5 to 7 minutes. Stir in roux.
Mix thoroughly. Reduce heat to medium and
begin stirring in heavy cream. Be sure to add
cream slowly so to keep cooking temperature
consistent. Stir in milk using the same method as
with the cream. Once incorporated, keep stirring
until the gravy begins to thicken; add salt and
any additional spices to taste. Continue stirring
frequently until gravy thickens, then reduce
heat to low and stir occasionally until desired
consistency is reached.

Serve immediately on biscuits with the fried
chicken, or store in the refrigerator for gravy
shots at your next party.

Finish the chicken: Heat oil to 350°F. Fry chicken
until golden brown and delicious, 8 to 10 minutes.
We recommend a cast-iron skillet for frying.

To serve: Place four biscuit bottoms on a work
surface. Place chicken on a biscuit, followed by
the bacon. Pour gravy over the bacon, and place
a fried egg and the cheddar on top. Cover with
the biscuit top.

Beast

5425 NORTHEAST 30TH AVENUE
(503) 841-6968
WWW.BEASTPDX.COM
CHEF AND OWNER: NAOMI POMEROY

Beast is one of the best restaurants in Portland. *Iron Chef* star Naomi Pomeroy is a fiery and charming woman who knows her way around a professional kitchen, chatting and laughing with her staff and listening to music on full blast. Memorable meals are prepared in this twenty-six-seat small and simple space. The restaurant has only two tables, so communal dining is the only way to go. It's fun chatting with the other people at the table and sharing the wonderful dining experience. There are quotations all over the walls, including a recipe for crème fraîche dough, which I have copied down and intend to make some time soon.

There are two seatings nightly, and it is a six-course meal. Dinners often start with a soup, which is followed by a house-made charcuterie plate consisting of tiny bites of wonderful foods—steak tartare, quail egg toast, and *tête de cochon,* a savory foie gras bonbon, just to name a few. Everything is local and seasonal, the cheese course is possibly the best in town, and on my last visit the plum beignets served with fresh ginger ice cream was scrumptious. If you splurge and go with the wine pairings, it is a meal you will not soon forget.

On Sundays, to the delight of countless Portlanders, Pomeroy serves brunch. Like dinner at Beast, there are two seatings, and the meal consists of four delectable courses. In addition to getting Sundays off to a grand start, Beast offers the monthly Recession Session, where the restaurant serves three-course meals for a fraction of the regular dinner price.

SUMMER VEGETABLE & DUNGENESS CRAB HASH

(SERVES 6)

2 tablespoons canola oil
4 medium-size waxy potatoes
4 ears of corn
½ yellow onion
½ pint cherry tomatoes
2 small handfuls of green beans
2 strips of good bacon
Salt and black pepper to taste
½ pound crabmeat, picked clean

For the hollandaise:

4 large egg yolks
2 teaspoons high-quality sherry vinegar
1 tablespoon boiling water
½ cup unsalted butter, melted and cooled to
    room temperature
½ teaspoon truffle salt
6–8 duck eggs*
6 good-quality bread slices, toasted (whole grain)

It is a good idea to poach an extra one or two eggs, just in case one breaks.

Dice the potatoes, squaring off the edges. Cook the potatoes in salted water until tender but not falling apart. Run under cold water to stop the cooking process. Cut the corn off the cobs, dice the onion, halve the cherry tomatoes, blanch the green beans in well-salted water, and run under cold water. Cut the beans into ¾-inch-long pieces. Cut the bacon into a ½-inch dice. Set everything in individual small bowls.

In a large frying pan, cook the bacon and onion. Add the potatoes (adding a little more oil if needed). After the potatoes get some color (shake constantly), add a little salt and pepper.

Add the green beans, tomatoes, and corn right away (they shouldn't cook, but they do need to get hot). Carefully add the crabmeat; be sure to keep the pieces as big as possible.

After the hash is done, you can put it aside. Heat the oven to 400°F (for a quick toast of your bread) and place the hash in the oven to rewarm when you need it.

Prepare the hollandaise: Whisk yolks with sherry vinegar. Slowly add boiling water, until ribbon stage (the yolks become pale and warmed).

Place mixture In a lightly boiling bain marie and whisk until tripled in volume. Remove bowl and double boiler from the heat—keep bowl on top of warm water—and continue to whisk.

While whisking, slowly add the room-temperature melted butter.

Remove the bowl after all the butter is incorporated. Adjust seasoning with truffle salt and an extra dash of sherry vinegar if needed.

Prepare the eggs: Poach the eggs in vinegary water (water with a drop or two of white vinegar) that has boiled but then been turned to medium heat. Poach the eggs by placing them in individual ramekins and gently dipping them into the water to turn them out. (You can poach the eggs ahead of time, as long as the yolk is still very soft. You can place them back in the water for a second to rewarm.) Don't mess with them until you think they are almost done so they don't break.

To serve: Plate the hash and serve with toast. Place a poached egg on top and finish with hollandaise and truffle salt.

COUNTRY CAT

7937 SOUTHEAST STARK STREET
(503) 408-1414
WWW.THECOUNTRYCAT.NET
CHEF AND OWNERS: ADAM AND JACKIE SAPPINGTON

The up-and-coming neighborhood Montevilla is home to some good eating places, and Country Cat ranks among the finest. Chef Adam Sappington and his wife, Jackie, serve up some of the best brunches, lunches, and dinners in Portland. Adam grew up in central Missouri and spent hours in the kitchen cooking with his mom and grandma. The love of family and the love of food brought Adam and Jackie to open Country Cat, with a menu that dedicates itself to serving hearty comfort food with strong and gutsy flavors.

The corner restaurant is cozy and friendly, and it is not unusual to see large families digging into the Country Cat's Whole Hog plate, consisting of rolled pork belly, a boneless loin chop, and smoked shoulder with perfect grits. Another spectacular large plate is the red wine braised beef on a spring onion bread salad with bacon vinaigrette. Although Country Cat is a destination for families, it is also a place to go alone, sit with some sort of reading device, and linger over an incredible dessert, like the trio of puddings with freshly baked cookies, the perfect way to end a meal.

Fried chicken with spoon bread is one of the most popular brunch items. Filling and hearty—the ultimate food to soothe and satisfy—the dish comes with two perfectly fried pieces of chicken and a big piece of spoon bread. It sits on the plate, daring you to eat it all.

For spoon bread to be just right, it needs to be light, somewhat custardy, with a crisp top—called spoon bread because it's so delicate it can be eaten with a spoon. Fried chicken, at its best, needs to be tender, flavorful, and crunchy.

Pecan Spoon Bread

(SERVES 8–10)

6 slices bacon, cut into lardons

2 teaspoons butter

⅓ cup sliced yellow onion

2¼ cups flour

2¼ teaspoons baking powder

1½ teaspoons salt

¼ teaspoon cayenne

1¼ teaspoons baking soda

1½ cups cornmeal

5 eggs

3 tablespoons sugar

4½ cups milk

1½ teaspoons white vinegar

2¼ cups heavy cream

1 cup chopped pecans, toasted

Special equipment: Bain-marie (water bath)

Preheat the oven to 350°F. Cook the bacon in butter; when almost crisp add the sliced onions and sweat. Strain and reserve fat. Set the bacon mixture aside. Mix together the dry ingredients in a large bowl and set aside. Mix the eggs, sugar, milk, and vinegar in a separate bowl. Add the reserved bacon fat. Fat should equal about ¼ cup.

Pour the wet mixture into the dry mixture and stir to incorporate. Stir in the bacon and onions. Pour batter into a greased 9 x 13-inch pan.

In a separate bowl whip cream to medium peaks and dollop over the top of the pudding. Cover and cook in the bain-marie (or if you don't have a bain-marie then place a smaller pot in a larger pot that contains hot water) in the preheated oven until it's set, about 1½ hours. After 1 hour, top the pudding with chopped pecans. The pudding is done when the center is just set but not dry. Let it stand for about 20 minutes before cutting.

Voodoo Doughnut
Multiple Locations
(503) 241-4704
voodoodoughnut.com

Talk about "keeping Portland weird." This popular bumper sticker motto might have been created after a trip to Voodoo Doughnut, the famous and pretty bizarre Portland doughnut shop. Lines form out the door at odd hours of the day or night, and the newly upgraded shop on the west side has all sorts of stuff that you can buy so you never forget this doughnut experience. Another way to remember it is to get married there. A real wedding, with doughnuts and coffee for six people, will cost you about $300. Try the assortments, which include some unusual toppings and flavors—and shapes. The cream-filled doughnut shaped like a phallus is very popular, as are the round doughnuts topped with Cap'n Crunch or Froot Loops, and a personal favorite, the maple bacon. My son, Nick, who eats bacon on anything, said it was "a damn good doughnut." And don't panic—there are vegan doughnuts, too.

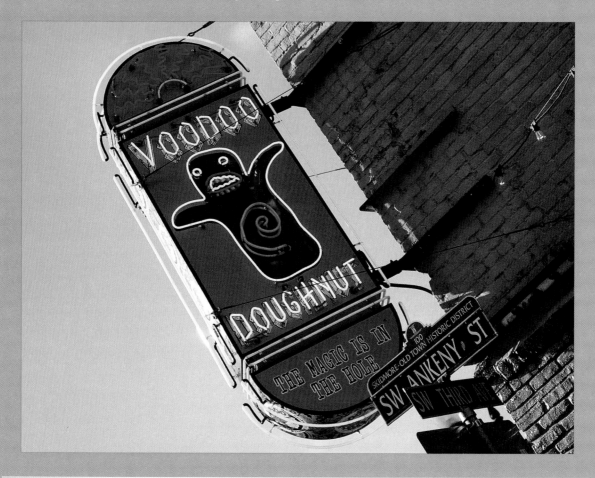

BAKERY BAR

2935 NORTHEAST GLISAN STREET
(503) 477-7779
WWW.BAKERYBAR.COM
OWNER AND CAKE DESIGNER: JOCELYN BARDA
HEAD BAKER: SAM LAMONT

This gem of a place, open daily until 2:00 p.m., serves some of the best breakfasts and baked goods in Portland. Airy and bright, with lots of covered outdoor seating, it's a great place to go to order a special occasion cake or dozens of cupcakes that will taste as good as they look. And they look good. For my husband's birthday, I ordered a mixed box of three dozen, and they all met my high expectations.

The kitchen is big and modern, and the atmosphere reflects the warmth of the delightful owner and master decorator, Jocelyn Barda. You won't lack for choices in baked goods, and the vegan options do much to raise the bar in that hard-to-achieve baked greatness category. The barista creates magic with the patterns of foam on the lattes and cappuccinos, using delicious Stumptown coffee. The scones are great, with a particular shout-out to the coconut scone, which is mesmerizing. And one bite of their extraordinary homemade jam on a biscuit or scone will blow you away.

Breakfasts are equally delicious, including the eggs, sandwiches, and pastries. Everything is baked daily at Bakery Bar, and you'll enjoy all of the offerings. Migas, when done right, is the best breakfast. This recipe is a keeper.

Migas

(SERVES 4 GENEROUSLY)

2 tablespoons canola oil

1 cup chorizo (see recipe below; you'll have more than you need and can freeze the rest and use later; also available at most supermarkets)

1 red onion, peeled and julienned

2 whole or 16 slices of pickled jalapeño (Bakery Bar pickles it in-house with garlic and rosemary)

4 good handfuls of broken tortilla chips

¼ cup spice mix (see recipe below)

10–12 large eggs cracked into a bowl and beaten with a fork until well combined

½ cup Cotija cheese

2 cups tomatillo salsa (see recipe below; you'll have more than you need and can use the rest later)

For the chorizo: (Makes 1½ pounds)

1½ teaspoons paprika

1½ teaspoons dried basil

¾ teaspoon chili powder

2¼ teaspoons kosher salt

¼ teaspoon cinnamon

2¼ teaspoons brown sugar

¼ cup canola oil

¼ pound ground pork

For the tomatillo salsa: (Makes 4 cups)

2 tablespoons canola or olive oil

2½ pounds fresh tomatillos, quartered or halved

1 large yellow onion, roughly chopped

2–3 fresh jalapeños, seeded and roughly chopped

1 tablespoon kosher salt

3 tablespoons brown sugar

½ teaspoon sherry vinegar

1 tablespoon apple cider vinegar

2¼ teaspoons ground cumin

2¼ teaspoons chili powder

½ teaspoon black pepper

Special equipment: Food processor

For the migas spice mix: (Makes 1 cup)

2 tablespoons paprika

2 tablespoons dried basil

1 tablespoon chili powder

3 tablespoons kosher salt

1 teaspoon cinnamon

3 tablespoons brown sugar

Heat oil in a skillet over a medium flame. Add the chorizo and cook until browned and crumbled. Add the onions and continue sautéing until the onions begin to soften.

Add pickled jalapeños and broken tortilla chips. Sprinkle with the spice mixture. Pour the beaten eggs into the skillet and let the eggs cook undisturbed until they begin to set, then stir them off the bottom of the pan gently, using a rubber spatula. Sprinkle in half of the Cotija cheese and continue cooking until the eggs are set.

Spoon onto a serving platter or individual plates.

Spoon the cooled tomatillo salsa over the top of the eggs and sprinkle with the rest of the Cotija cheese.

To make the chorizo: In a bowl combine all dry ingredients with the oil. Add the pork and mix well.

To make the salsa: Preheat the oven to 375°F. On a sheet pan, toss the tomatillos, onions, and peppers with the oil. Cook for 25 to 30 minutes, or until soft.

Cool and process in a food processor with the rest of the ingredients.

To make the spice mix: Combine all ingredients. Store in an airtight container.

BAKERY BAR BISCUITS

Sam LaMont has worked at Bakery Bar since 2006. She now runs the baking operation there and manages the baking staff. The biscuit recipe is from her mother, Paula LaMont, who is from the South. They are both amazing cooks, bakers, and artists. Here is their perfect recipe for the perfect biscuit:

BISCUITS

(MAKES 10–12 BISCUITS)

2 cups all-purpose flour
3 teaspoons baking powder
1 teaspoon salt
1 teaspoon sugar
½ cup butter, right out of the refrigerator
1 egg
⅔ cup buttermilk
Melted butter (to finish)

Preheat the oven to 350°F. Whisk all dry ingredients together in a bowl to evenly blend. If incorporating any flavors, such as pepper, herbs, or zest, add them in this step. Cut in butter with a cutter or knives (we use a bench scraper). You want to keep your hands off the butter since this will melt it. Cut in until the sizes vary from pea size to almost dime size. In a separate bowl, whisk together the egg and buttermilk.

Pour the egg-buttermilk into the dry ingredients, and using a bowl scraper or a rubber spatula, gently fold the liquid into the dry until almost mixed in. Finish the mixing on the table. Lightly flour your work surface, and turn the dough out onto the surface. Lightly sprinkle a bit of flour onto the surface of the dough, too. Pat the dough out to about 2 inches thick, incorporating any dry ingredients that haven't mixed in. Using a bench scraper, gently fold the dough in half, using the scraper to pick up half of it and fold over (it will be too sticky to lift without the scraper). Pat out again and repeat. Add flour, as needed, a sprinkle at a time, and continue to fold and pat four or five times until the dough is neither too dry nor too wet. You want a gentle hand, and too much flour will make the biscuits tough. Pat out a final time to about 1¼ inches.

Use a floured round cutter (2¼ x 2½ inches). Place biscuits a good 3 inches apart on a sheet pan. Brush with melted butter. Bake in the preheated oven for approximately 20 minutes, maybe more, rotating halfway though until a nice golden brown crust forms.

Broder

2508 Southeast Clinton Street
(503) 736-3333
www.BroderPDX.com
Chef: Derek Hanson
Owner: Peter Bro

I fell in love with Broder on my first visit. I was there for a photo shoot for *Portland Monthly* magazine. The restaurant, which opened in 2007, is in a favorite Portland neighborhood, the Clinton area, which is small and has just the right amount of places to do your shopping, drinking, and eating. Part of the charm of Broder, in addition to all the cute Swedish plates and skillets, is the manager of the restaurant, Joe Conklin, who is the sweetest, most adorable guy in Portland. He couldn't be friendlier or more helpful, and he can do fifty things at once, all perfectly, with a huge smile on his face.

Broder is very small, cozy, and charming. The kitchen is tiny, and the selection of Scandinavian-style food is fabulous. *Bords* (literally wooden boards) hold, for example, brown bread and rye crisp, cured meat, smoked trout, Swedish cheese, a clementine with yogurt fruit, and roasted apple. It's a great meal. We enjoy the baked scrambles, with gravlax, as well as wild mushrooms and smoked trout with horseradish cream. There's also the excellent club sandwich with gravlax. Broder does Swedish meatballs right; they are tender and great with lingonberry jam.

But a favorite dish—and I am certainly not alone in this—is the aebleskiver, the fluffiest, most extraordinary pancakes, served with your choice of two of the following: homemade lemon curd, maple syrup, lingonberry jam, or house-made applesauce. You can smell them cooking, along with all the other tasty and soul-warming dishes Broder serves.

Broder has recently begun concentrating on dinner as well, and we are all expecting some terrific meals, Swedish style.

Baked Eggs with Hash

(SERVES 4)

For the hash:

4 Yukon gold potatoes, diced
1 red bell pepper, diced
1 green bell pepper, diced
1 red onion, peeled and diced
½ bunch green onions, thinly sliced
2 tablespoons olive oil
Salt and black pepper to taste

For the eggs:

2 tablespoons butter
8 large eggs
Heavy cream
Salt and black pepper to taste

Preheat the oven to 400°F. In a medium bowl combine the potatoes, peppers, onion, and green onions. Toss with the olive oil. Salt and pepper to taste.

Roast in the preheated oven until potatoes are tender, approximately 35 minutes. Store for use right away or keep in refrigerator for a few days.

Prepare the eggs: Preheat the oven to 400°F. Coat a cast-iron skillet with pan spray or butter. For each serving, crack 2 fresh eggs at a time into the pan and add 1 tablespoon of heavy cream. Salt and pepper to taste.

Bake in the preheated oven on bottom rack for 6 to 7 minutes or until whites are solid.

To finish: Meanwhile, heat 2 tablespoons of butter in a large frying pan. Add the hash mixture along with your favorite ingredients. Fry until heated through. Try it Broder-style with diced ham and roast beef, or a veggie treat with spinach and mushrooms.

Serve in bowls or shallow plates and top with the fresh baked eggs.

Sandwiches

When I attended the Culinary Institute of America some years back, we had a three-week class devoted to the sandwich. I remember, as if it were yesterday, the hour-long lecture and demo on the BLT. We studied the order of the ingredients, perfect mayonnaise placement, and on and on until the finale, which concluded with a diagonal cut and a frilly toothpick. Sandwiches, though tasty, were predictable and more convenient than creative.

Since that time there's evolved a new appreciation and energy devoted to the sandwich. Although it is possible to get an absolutely extraordinary grilled cheese at Sunshine Tavern or Bunk, both places serve sandwiches that scream with creativity and, at times, brilliance.

With the modern focus of using the best ingredients available in small and large plates, based on seasonality and locale, sandwiches garner the same attention.

These lunch dishes are no longer a couple of slices of bread slapped with some sliced meat or cheese and a spread of either mayonnaise, ketchup, or mustard. Instead, the choices of spectacular bread are too numerous to count; the same with the toppings and local produce. The rise in the house-made charcuterie has brought spectacular pâtés and sausages, and local cheese-makers have gotten into the act as well. The astounding availability of all these products, perfectly prepared, makes for some pretty great sandwiches. Portland has the sandwich down.

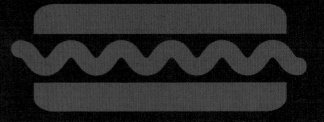

Cheese Bar

6031 Southeast Belmont Street
(503) 222-6014
WWW.CHEESE-BAR.COM
Owner: Steve Jones
Chef: Timothy Daly

The laidback Cheese Bar has a wide variety of cheeses, some hard to find, like burrata and mountina, as well as some more standard favorites at their peak of ripe perfection. They have reasonably priced, well-chosen wines by the glass and some excellent beer from small local breweries. The two guys at the helm, Steve Jones and Chef Timothy Daly, run their business in an easygoing and super-friendly manner. Their style is simple comfort food, reflected in their pressed sandwiches, like the panini-grilled mac-n-cheese (which is amazing), and desserts like bread pudding and fruit crumbles. Diners and delivery people alike are treated like old friends, and Jones and Daly personally offer

tastes and suggestions. The experience is delightful, the kind of place that makes you feel so comfortable you end up staying much longer than you need to. Everyone seems to be having a great time.

Cheese Bar has a small menu, but everything on it is fantastic. The coconut cauliflower soup is creamy curried deliciousness, and the sandwiches are some of the best in Portland. Daly is a master of ingredient pairings, and each component gets to shine in its own cheesy, beefy, or porky way. Before you head out the door, be sure to grab one of the honeymoon bars, chewy, dense-yet-cakey squares of dried fruits, nuts, and other ingredients, or the same bar with the addition of chopped chocolate and coconut, called Almond Joy. And it is.

Northwest Tuna Melt

(SERVES 1)

For roast garlic mayonnaise:

1½ cups mayonnaise
1 large clove garlic, chopped
Zest from ½ lemon (¼–½ teaspoon)
1 tablespoon fresh basil
½ tablespoon lemon juice
½ tablespoon fresh oregano
Pinch of salt

Quality line-caught Oregon albacore tuna* or small can or jar of the best-quality chunk fillet of tuna, flaked in large pieces, drained
2 tablespoons roast garlic mayonnaise
2 tablespoons sweet pickle relish
2 ounces quality sharp white cheddar (your favorite), sliced thin
2 slices whole wheat levain (sourdough)
Assorted pickled vegetables (for garnish)

* Canned is acceptable, but if you are ambitious, you could poach your own fresh-caught tuna in olive oil. Yum.

To make the garlic mayonnaise: In a food processor, process until smooth. Keep covered in refrigerator.

Gently mix in just enough garlic mayonnaise with the tuna to hold everything together; try not to break up all the chunks too much.

Spread the mayonnaise on one slice of bread.

Spoon the relish on the other slice.

Place slices of cheese on both slices of bread, achieving maximum coverage.

Place a good layer of tuna salad onto one side, and close the sandwich.

Grill on a panini press or in a sauté pan until golden brown, toasty hot, melted, and fragrant.

Garnish with a variety of pickled veggies on the side and dig in. (Don't forget a side of chips—this sandwich demands them.)

MAC-N-CHEESE

Although Cheese Bar is mostly about sandwiches and great goods to go, I could not resist asking these kind gentlemen for the recipe for the panini-grilled mac-n-cheese. This dish is too good to be true. Caution: Could be habit-forming. This recipe yields 12 ½-pound portions.

For the sauce:

4 tablespoons unsalted butter
¼–⅓ cup flour (more or less to make a tight roux)
1 quart whole milk
1–2 teaspoons salt
½ teaspoon pepper
¼ teaspoon smoked paprika
1 large yellow onion, small dice
2 tablespoons olive oil
5 cloves garlic, minced
½ pound sharp white cheddar
½ pound Danish Havarti (or other semi-firm, tasty melting cheese)
¼ pound Parmigiano Reggiano (or other very aged, dry, flavorful grating cheese)
1 pound (5-ounce) elbow macaroni, cooked in salt water and drained
1–2 cups soft bread crumbs

In a large saucepan, melt the butter and mix in flour, to make a tight roux. Cook for several minutes, stirring, until light golden brown.

Slowly add the milk, stirring frequently, until thick and beginning to boil.

Season the sauce with the spices.

In a large saucepan, cook the onion in the olive oil until slightly caramelized; add garlic and cook for 1 minute.

Stir the onions into the béchamel sauce.

Preheat the oven to 350°F. Grate all the cheeses and mix. Reserve 1 cup for the top.

In a very large bowl combine all the ingredients, including the cooked pasta, except the bread crumbs and the reserved cup of cheese.

Split the mixture evenly among 2 buttered 9 x 13-inch baking pans, lined with parchment.

Sprinkle with the cheese. Bake for 15 to 20 minutes, until hot, melted, bubbly, and maybe a bit browned on top.

Cool in pan. When fully cool, remove the mac and cheese in one piece, discard the parchment and cut each pan into 12 portions (2 x 6 inches), allowing for 12 total servings from the entire recipe.

Lightly coat each mac stick with bread crumbs. Griddle breaded mac on panini press or in heavy-bottomed sauté pan over medium heat until golden brown, crusty, and hot throughout. Serve with a simple side salad.

Salami Milano, Mountina Cheese & Mama Lil's

(SERVES 1)

Slaw (see recipe below):

½ ounce Mama Lil's marinated spicy Italian peppers (or other favorite oil-marinated slightly spicy peppers)

1½ ounces Mountina cheese (or Muenster), sliced medium thin

1½ ounces Italian salami, sliced medium thin

Mustard red wine vinaigrette (see recipe below)

1 demi baguette, sliced in half lengthwise

Build the sandwich with a layer of Mama Lil's peppers on the bottom, cheese, meat, and slaw on top of the baguette.

For the slaw:

1 napa cabbage leaf, sliced thin
2 radicchio leaves, sliced thin
1 tablespoon pickled fennel, sliced
1 tablespoon roasted red onions
Salt and black pepper to taste

Combine all ingredients in a bowl and season with salt and pepper.

To finish: Dress lightly with zesty mustard red wine vinaigrette and top the sandwich with slaw. Grill the sandwich in a pan to warm through and toast the demi baguette, but not necessarily to melt the cheese.

For the mustard red wine vinaigrette: (Yields 1 quart)

3 shallots, minced
7 garlic cloves, minced
2 red jalapeños, minced with some seeds
3 sprigs oregano
3 sprigs thyme
3 sprigs marjoram
1 cup red wine vinegar
3 tablespoons whole grain mustard
½ cup lemon juice
1½ teaspoons salt
1½ teaspoons black pepper
2 cups canola oil
½ cup extra-virgin olive oil

Finely chop shallots, garlic, jalapeños, and herbs.

In a food processor, combine remaining ingredients except the olive oil. Slowly drizzle in the oil while running the blender to achieve emulsification.

Roasted Zucchini, Red Pepper, Onion, Olive Tapenade & Goat Cheese Sandwich

(SERVES 1)

Zucchini sliced into thin (1/8-inch) strips, lengthwise
1 red onion, bisect from pole to pole, skin, remove root
    core, slice into ¼-inch-thick wedges
¼ cup olive oil
2 tablespoons balsamic vinegar
Salt and black pepper to taste

For the pepper:

1 red bell pepper
1 tablespoon olive oil
Salt and black pepper to taste

For the olive tapenade:

1 cup mixed marinated olives, pitted
1–2 anchovy fillets
¼ bunch thyme, stemmed, chopped fine
¼ bunch Italian parsley, stemmed, chopped fine
1 lemon, zest and juice
1–3 cloves garlic, minced
2–3 tablespoons extra-virgin olive oil
Black pepper to taste

To serve:

4 tablespoons goat cheese
3–5 fresh basil leaves
2 slices whole wheat levain (sourdough or other
    hearty artisan bread of your choice)

Preheat the oven to 350°F. Marinate the zucchini and onions by tossing in a bowl with olive oil and balsamic vinegar to coat. Season well with salt and pepper.

Place a sheet pan or cookie sheet into the oven for 5 to 8 minutes.

Pour the marinated vegetables onto the hot sheet pan and spread into an even layer. Return vegetables to the oven and roast for 10 to 12 minutes, until cooked through (juices are released and mostly cooked off). You can stir vegetables, as edges of the pan will cook faster, and rotate or change the pan's oven position, depending on your oven, for even roasting.

Remove the pan from the oven and allow vegetables to cool on the pan.

Prepare the pepper: Slice the pepper in half, core and seed, and cut into quarters.

Toss the pepper in olive oil, salt, and pepper and roast under a broiler, skin side up, until charred (about 8 to 10 minutes).

Remove from the oven, put in a bowl, and cover while still hot to steam skins.

Remove the charred skin when the pepper is cool.

To make the tapenade: Pulse all ingredients in a food processor until chopped fine but not pureed.

To serve: Spread soft cheese in a generous layer on one slice of bread, then a layer of basil leaves. Spread olive tapenade on the other slice.

Layer the veggies for maximum coverage.

Grill the sandwich on a panini press until golden, hot, and melted.

Halve, and serve with a frosty beverage and some chips.

Olympic Provisions

West Side
1632 Northwest Thurman Street
(503) 894-8136
Chef: Erin Williams

East Side
107 Southeast Washington Street
(503) 954-3663
Olympicprovisions.com
Chef: Alex Yoder

Olympic Provisions is a PDX hot spot for awesome restaurant food as well as for selling excellent "made in Portland" charcuterie. Salumist Elias Cairo is a master of all things cured and smoked, and many of the charcuterie plates in town use the Olympic Provisions products. There are two locations, both of which function as restaurants and factories. The one on the east side is moody, with its cement and dark wood, and the other on the west side is the opposite—stainless, pale woods, glass, and sun-filled. The food at both is great, from soups to dessert.

The sandwiches are in the top five in Portland, and many of the sandwiches are porky and strictly for carnivores, but this particular delicious sandwich is actually targeted to the Montessori school down the street. It is a banana, seasonal jam, and Nocciolata sandwich, and believe me, while targeted at them, it is not just for school kids. This sandwich is also a favorite of Chef Erin Williams, and we have spent probably too much time discussing what a superb combination of flavors and textures come together here. Nocciolata is a wonderful product, and pairing with the other ingredients is sheer ecstasy. What a decadent delight. Olympic Provisions gets its bread from Lovejoy Bakers, which is one of the components that make this sandwich extraordinary.

Before you leave, get a bunch of the house-made hot dogs to go. They are the best in town.

PORCHETTA SANDWICH

(SERVES 4)

1 2-pound pork belly, skin removed

For the brine:

1 gallon water

1 cup kosher salt

½ cup white granulated sugar

6 bay leaves

2 tablespoons black peppercorns

2 tablespoons fennel seed

2 tablespoons chile flakes

½–¾ pound loose Italian sausage

2 tablespoons olive oil

Chicken or meat broth

Combine brine ingredients and bring to a boil. Cool to room temperature. Submerge belly in the brine and refrigerate for 24 hours. Drain off brine.

Spoon ½ to ¾ pound loose Italian sausage of your liking down the center of the belly. Roll the belly up tightly around the sausage and tie into a roast with kitchen twine.

Preheat the oven to 350°F. Heat a wide, heavy-bottomed pan or wide pot over medium-high heat and add about 2 tablespoons of olive oil to coat the bottom of the pan. Place the porchetta roast in the pan and sear well on all sides, browning evenly. When roast is seared, place it in a roasting pan and tent loosely with foil. Place the pan in the oven and roast until the porchetta reaches an internal temperature of 135°F. Take out of the oven and cool. Chill thoroughly in the refrigerator overnight.

Slice the chilled porchetta into desired thickness. Heat slices in 1 or 2 inches of chicken or meat broth or lightly salted water, until slices are cooked through, tender, and delicious. Serve on your favorite bread and prepare yourself for a fine porchetta sandwich.

Note: If you bring the roast up to 165°F, you can slice and serve it as a main course. Chilled slices of porchetta can also be pan-seared in fat.

BLT

(SERVES 1)

4 strips of good-quality bacon

2 slices of bread (such as country levain/sourdough)

2–3 tablespoons mayonnaise

Several leaves of mixed lettuces and/or chicories,
    such as radicchio

2 slices of large, ripe tomato

Salt and black pepper to taste

Fry the bacon to desired crispness. Meanwhile, toast the bread. Slather both pieces of toast with mayonnaise, and lay the lettuce on one piece. Layer tomato slices over lettuce and sprinkle with salt and pepper. Lay bacon over the tomato and top with the other piece of bread. Slice and serve.

NOCCIOLATA, BANANA & JAM SANDWICH

(SERVES 1)

2 slices bread, preferably country levain/sourdough,
    multigrain, or some other hearty or nutty type

2–3 tablespoons Nocciolata (or Nutella, if Nocciolata
    isn't available)

2–3 tablespoons good-quality jam or preserves,
    your favorite flavor

Sprinkling of sea salt

1 banana, cut into 7 or 8 thin slices

Toast the bread. Spread Nocciolata on one piece of bread and jam on the other. Sprinkle crunchy sea salt over the Nocciolata, then lay the banana slices over it. Top with the piece of toast with jam. Slice on the diagonal and serve.

ATE-OH-ATE

2454 EAST BURNSIDE STREET
(503) 445-6101
WWW.ATEOHATE.COM
CHEFS AND OWNERS: BEN DYER, JASON OWENS,
AND DAVID KREIFELS

On my last visit to Ate-Oh-Ate (the area code for Hawaii), I brought three friends from Seattle. They love Hawaiian food, and since we had dined the night before at Laurelhurst Market, which shares the same trio of owners, everyone was stoked. The room at Ate-Oh-Ate is simple and comfortable; the smells of the cooking food hit us as soon as we got out of our car.

I have not had a great deal of experience with Hawaiian food and was happy to be going with experts. Chef and owner Ben Dyer was born there, so we had additional reason for high expectations. We had the beef short ribs, island burger, katsu chicken, and hekka, which was a stir-fry with fresh vegetables, a fish cake, and excellent yam noodles. The entrees at Ate-Oh-Ate are served with very good macaroni salad and rice, and the portions are large, while the prices are not. The short ribs are tender perfection, and the island burger with crispy pork belly, avocado, shredded lettuce, and onion is tasty and a good item to share. Even I would have trouble with all that richness in one sitting.

Chef Ben Bettinger, of Beaker and Flask, stops in every Saturday for a musube, a seaweed, egg, and rice roll with a good-size chunk of grilled out-of-the-can Spam. Reluctantly, I tried one. I put it in the acquired taste category.

Try shaved ice for dessert, which hits the spot on a warm afternoon. Coconut ice cream is one of my favorites, and this one is particularly good. Ate-Oh-Ate is the perfect place to go for something different and full of flavor.

Shoyu Chicken Sandwich

(SERVES 4)

6 chicken thighs, bone-in with skin

1 cup soy sauce

½ cup brown sugar

3 tablespoons honey

⅔ cup chicken stock

1½ teaspoons hoisin sauce

1 star anise, crushed, or ¼ teaspoon five-spice powder

2 tablespoons ginger root, peeled and chopped

1 tablespoon unsalted butter

4 good-quality burger buns

4 teaspoons mayonnaise

For the coleslaw:

1 carrot, grated

1 cup grated green and red cabbage

3 tablespoons chopped pineapple

For the dressing:

1 tablespoon rice wine vinegar

5 tablespoons mayonnaise

1 tablespoon pineapple juice

1 teaspoon sesame oil

1½ teaspoons white sugar

Pinch of salt and black pepper

Preheat the oven to 300°F. Place the chicken in a 6 x 6-inch baking dish that can be placed over a flame.

In a medium bowl combine the remaining ingredients. Pour the sauce over the chicken. Cover the dish with foil and bake for 90 minutes, turning every half hour. The chicken is done when uniformly tender when pierced with the tip of a knife. It should not be falling apart.

Remove the chicken from the oven, take off the foil, and place in the refrigerator to cool. When the fat has risen to the top and solidified, scrape from the top of the chicken and remaining sauce.

Remove the meat from the pan. Place the pan over medium heat until liquid and strain into a saucepan. Simmer and reduce by half. Pick the meat off the bones and add the meat to the reduced sauce. Heat through and remove from flame.

In a medium bowl combine the carrot, cabbage, and pineapple for the slaw.

In a medium bowl whisk together all the ingredients for the dressing. Toss the slaw ingredients with the dressing.

Distribute the chicken evenly among the four buns. Top with the coleslaw.

Meat Cheese Bread

1406 Southeast Stark Street
(503) 234-1700
Chef and Owner: John Stewart

Meat Cheese Bread has been the talk of the town since it opened in 2008. Owner John Stewart has been cooking since he was fourteen in his hometown of Albuquerque, New Mexico. His experience in the kitchen ran the gamut from the town diner to some super upscale kitchens. During his culinary journey he realized his food philosophy. He loved and appreciated the tastes and sophistication of the labor-intensive kitchens but was not comfortable in that environment. He decided that he wanted to cook the short ribs and cure the salmon, but he wanted to do it in a simple place, and most importantly, he wanted it on a sandwich. Hence the simple name: Meat Cheese Bread.

All of the rolls and breads at Meat Cheese Bread are made in-house, even the perfectly flaky croissants. All the meats are cured and the vegetables pickled in this small restaurant. Mayonnaise is made from scratch, along with the soups and dressings. And it totally shows. The flank steak served on a roll with pickled onions and blue cheese aioli is a perfect example of Stewart's philosophy. The steak is served medium-rare with great flavor, and the blue cheese kicks it up a notch. Each sandwich is a phenomenal sum of its parts, and a sandwich as simple as egg salad reaches new heights. Served on a toasted house-made croissant, with perfectly crisp bacon, lettuce, and sweet onion, Meat Cheese Bread truly has achieved a perfect sandwich.

Park Kitchen Sandwich

(MAKES 4 SANDWICHES)

For the vinaigrette:

1 teaspoon Dijon mustard

1 pinch of kosher salt

¼ cup red wine

¾ cup sherry vinegar

2 cups canola oil

For the blue cheese aioli:

1 tablespoon whole grain mustard

1 clove garlic, minced

1 whole egg

1 tablespoon lemon juice

Salt to taste

2 cups canola oil

¼ cup crumbled blue cheese

For the pickled onions:

1 red onion cut in half lengthwise, skin on

¼ cup red wine vinegar

¼ cup sherry vinegar

¼ cup water

1 teaspoon kosher salt

4 ciabatta rolls

4 ounces salad greens

8 ounces grilled, cooled, and sliced flank steak

2 ounces crumbled blue cheese

4 sprigs picked and rough chopped Italian parsley

1 pinch each salt and black pepper

1 ounce sherry vinaigrette

4 ounces pickled onions (see recipe below)

4 tablespoons blue cheese aioli

To make the vinaigrette: In a medium bowl whisk together all the ingredients.

Prepare the blue cheese aioli: In a medium bowl whisk together the mustard, garlic, egg, lemon juice, and salt. Slowly drizzle in the oil while constantly whisking. Try to keep a thick consistency the entire time. When all the oil is added, fold or puree in the crumbled blue cheese.

Heat oven to 350°F.

Prepare the pickled onions: Place the red onion sliced face down in a small roasting pan, add the other ingredients, and bake uncovered for 30 minutes. The onion should give slightly when pushed. Let the onion cool in the juices, then peel and slice in thin strips lengthwise.

Assemble the sandwich: Split the four rolls open and place on a work surface. Combine the first 6 ingredients and toss.

Spread the underside of the top and bottom of the sandwich with the aioli. Place the steak and salad mixture evenly divided among the four sandwiches. Top with the pickled onions and then with the aioli.

BLUE HOUR

250 NORTHWEST 13TH AVENUE
(503) 226-3394
WWW.BLUEHOURONLINE.COM
EXECUTIVE CHEF: THOMAS BOYCE

Portland has been waiting for Thomas Boyce ever since it leaked out that he was coming to take the helm at the sophisticated Bruce Carey restaurant Blue Hour. Working as chef de cuisine for over fifteen years at the famed L.A. jewel of modern California cuisine, Spago, his move to PDX was eagerly anticipated. Thomas and family moved to Portland for a change of lifestyle and to allow his wife, Kim Boyce, a talented baker and winner of the James Beard award for her book *Good to the Grain,* to work on her own career. Kim Boyce is a former pastry chef (Spago and Campanile).

Chef Boyce is charming, and his youthful appearance belies his age, as he has been cooking for over twenty years. Blue Hour opened its doors in 2000 to rave reviews and quickly became one of the leading restaurants in the Pearl District.

The menu at Blue Hour has been rethought and refined, resulting in stellar food. The forty-two-year-old Boyce says with confidence: "I don't like fussy food. I like some complexity but not overdone. I'm seeing crudos ("raw" fish in Italian and Spanish) and

seafood, which is underutilized in the Portland scene. I'm seeing mostly French and Italian, my base, but pulling in some Japanese and Indian flavors. I love handmade pasta and want it to be special. Actually, I want everything to be special ... you look at the menu and have a hard time deciding."

The restaurant itself has a timeless elegance, with curtains that hang ceiling to floor and giant windows with lots of light. There is seating outside, and the place is always abuzz with local businesspeople or those who are just exploring the Pearl, an upscale neighborhood in a constant state of change. Since the space is essentially downstairs from perhaps the coolest advertising agency in the world, Weiden + Kennedy, this is a seriously intense and creative crowd. Even in inclement weather, people sit on the outside deck, warmed by heaters, sipping fine cocktails and eating food that is sublime.

Grilled Indian Spiced Lamb Sandwich

(SERVES 6)

1 clove garlic, crushed

1 teaspoon chopped ginger

2 teaspoons honey

Juice of 1 lime

1 tablespoon olive oil

A few sprigs of cilantro

4–5 mint leaves

½ cup plain yogurt

1 2-pound piece of boneless lamb

For the tomato chutney:

1 teaspoon cumin seed

1 teaspoon mustard seed

2 green cardamom pods

1 teaspoon vegetable oil

¼ tablespoon chopped garlic

½ tablespoon chopped ginger

1 finely chopped Serrano or jalapeño pepper

½ cup finely diced onion

Salt and black pepper to taste

3 cups peeled, seeded, and chopped tomatoes

¼ cup golden raisins, rehydrated with
    ¼ cup warm water

1 tablespoon brown sugar

1 tablespoon tamarind paste

For the pickled cauliflower:

1 head cauliflower, thinly sliced

1 carrot, thinly sliced

1 jalapeño, thinly sliced

1 tablespoon chopped garlic

1 tablespoon chopped ginger

½ teaspoon powdered turmeric

2 cardamom pods

3 cloves

1 bay leaf

½ tablespoon coriander seeds

1½ tablespoons kosher salt

½ cup sugar

1 cup champagne vinegar

1½ cups water

For assembly:

4–6 crusty rolls

4–6 handfuls of arugula or some other
    strongly flavored green

Marinated lamb, thinly sliced

Cauliflower

Pickled chutney

Puree all of the first set of ingredients except the lamb in a blender and blend until smooth. Cover the meat with the marinade and allow it to sit overnight in the refrigerator, then cook it until rare (135°F internal temperature).

To make the tomato chutney: In a small saucepan over medium heat, gently toast the spices. When aromatic, add the vegetable oil and let the spices sizzle for a few seconds, then add the garlic, ginger, chile pepper, and onion. Season with salt, and cook until tender.

Add the tomatoes, golden raisins, sugar, and tamarind paste. Cook on low heat for about 45 minutes or until the chutney has a thick consistency.

To make the pickled cauliflower: Combine vegetables and spices in a large bowl and season with salt. Let sit for 15 minutes.

Combine sugar, vinegar, and water in a small pot and cook until sugar is melted. Pour mixture over vegetable-spice mix and let sit for at least 2 hours before eating.

To assemble: Place the greens on the sandwiches and top with the lamb slices.

Spread the cauliflower over the meat and top with the chutney.

Bunk Bar

Multiple Locations
www.BunkSandwiches.com
Chef and Owners: Tommy Habetz and Nick Wood

The word spread fast when the first Bunk opened its doors in November 2008. Partners Tommy Habetz and Nick Wood, both chefs of considerable note (Habetz worked with Mario Batali, and Wood earned his stripes at Brennan's in New Orleans), looked at the food scene in Portland, factored in the state of the economy, and decided to take their extraordinary talents in a whole new direction. Although it is not at all difficult to find a good sandwich in PDX, there are not many places devoted to nothing but. Bunk Sandwiches and Bunk Bar have chosen their top-quality ingredients carefully, with the chefs dealing personally with the local farmers and vendors used by the most upscale restaurants in town. Bunk Sandwiches—the first Bunk—is minute, and it's not unusual to see the line forming out the door. There is some seating, but many grab their grub and eat it elsewhere.

When Bunk Bar opened in the summer of 2010, it was a dream come true for the people who were used to waiting in line. The place is huge, with pinball machines, lounge chairs, sofas, comfy booths, and a big bar. A giant mural on the wall pays homage to the movie *Paris, Texas,* one of Habetz's favorites. Habetz, by the way, is so friendly and warm, that his places couldn't be any other way. And mellow and totally chill Wood is equally welcoming and delightful. The third Bunk, which opened in 2011, is small, cozy, and serving the same high-quality grub as its older siblings.

Honestly, Bunk sandwiches are so bewitching, the place could be housed in apple boxes in a windowless basement, and it would still get the crowds. Every sandwich is prepared with the same attention that both Habetz and Wood paid to the food at the upscale white-tablecloth restaurants where they perfected their artistry. Their meatball Parmesan hero is the best in town, and the shrimp po'boy has a tasty combination of textures. There are always some out-of-this world desserts to choose from; in particular, the mini fruit pies and assorted whoopee pies always hit the spot.

BURGERVILLE

This fast food chain has been in business in the Northwest for over fifty years. It is unlike any other fast food chain. The menu is seasonal and the company works with local farmers and sustainable partners to provide food that is good; in other words, you don't feel like you are doing your body, or soul, any damage.

Local vegetarian-fed and antibiotic-free beef is used in the burgers, and cage-free eggs in breakfast offerings. Salads offer mixed greens topped with smoked salmon and Oregon hazelnuts. Sides and desserts rely on seasonal, local ingredients, like the hand-prepared buttermilk-battered onion rings made from Walla Walla, sweet onions grown in Washington and Oregon, and the blackberry or pumpkin milkshakes. In the spring, Burgerville offers fabulous battered asparagus spears with a garlic aioli, and store-made lemonade with fresh berries. Summers bring strawberry shortcake, with buttermilk, sweet cream, and unsalted butter from a local dairy.

Roasted Cauliflower Sandwich

(SERVES 4)

1 head cauliflower, cut into chunks or slices
½ red onion, sliced thin
4 cloves garlic, chopped
1 tablespoon chile flakes
2 tablespoons red wine vinegar
¼ cup olive oil
Salt to taste

For the salsa verde:

½ shallot, diced
2 tablespoons red wine vinegar
1 head Italian parsley
1 bunch tarragon
A few mint leaves
2 anchovy fillets
1 tablespoon Dijon mustard
1 clove garlic
½ cup extra-virgin olive oil

For assembly:

1 bunch arugula, cleaned
4 ciabatta rolls, split and brushed with a little olive oil

Preheat the oven to 450°F. On a large baking sheet with sides, toss together all the ingredients and roast until caramelized and tender, approximately 15 to 20 minutes.

Prepare the salsa verde: Macerate the shallot in the red wine vinegar for a few minutes. Add the rest of the ingredients and puree in a food processor or blender.

To assemble: Grill the ciabatta rolls until toasted. Toss the arugula with the salsa verde. Add about a cup of cauliflower and some arugula to each roll. Enjoy.

Sunshine Tavern

3111 Southeast Division Street
(503) 688-1750
www.SunshinePDX.com
Chef and Owners: Jenn Louis and David Welch

Sunshine Tavern, the recently launched 2011 sibling to the extremely delicious restaurant Lincoln (see page 22), feels like an old-time luncheonette, but with really good food and lots of terrific alcohol, including margaritas from a frozen drink machine. The place is all windows; it's beautifully designed, with a style mix of sophisticated and funky.

A shuffleboard table in the center and a couple of arcade games lend a certain charm, along with the counters at both the bar and in front of the open kitchen. The menu is casual but continues to represent Jenn Louis's flair for ingredient pairing, keeping things fresh, seasonal, and always interesting. The food at Sunshine is more casual than at Lincoln, as it should be—it is a tavern—with great salads, sandwiches, and awesome griddled burgers. The restaurant, which opens at 5:00 p.m., has some excellent starters, such as Italian pork sausage, gravy cheese fries, and creamy and delicious chicken liver mousse with toasted baguette. The candied hazelnuts are a swell little snack, and who doesn't love garlic toast?

The terrific pizzas (particularly the roasted asparagus, red onion, garlic, and Fontina cheese) and the fried chicken and waffles are just right. Egg dishes from the brunch menu include a couple of my favorites in town. Baked eggs with chickpeas, spinach, anchovy, tomatoes, and garlic are served with quintessential hash browns, and the hangtown frittata with fried oysters and pork belly draws me in monthly.

The soft-serve ice cream, from Sunshine's very own machine, is a welcome change of pace, and when it's topped with hazelnut crunch, it is legendary. Ricotta doughnuts sprinkled with ginger sugar are the perfect complement to a superb cup of Ristretto coffee. And not to be missed is the spectacular Murphy's Irish stout float. Jenn and David have done it again.

MONTE CRISTO

(SERVES 2)

1 quart oil for frying, or as needed

⅔ cup water

1 egg

⅔ cup all-purpose flour

1¾ teaspoons baking powder

1 teaspoon salt

½ teaspoon ground black pepper

4 slices brioche

6 thin slices turkey

6 thin slices ham

4 thin slices Swiss cheese

2 large eggs

2 tablespoons olive oil

Maldon salt to taste

4 tablespoons powdered sugar

Marionberry preserves

Special equipment: Deep fryer

Heat 5 inches of oil in a deep fryer to 365°F. While oil is heating, make the batter: In a medium bowl whisk together the water and egg. Combine the flour, baking powder, salt, and pepper; whisk into the egg mixture until smooth. Set aside in the refrigerator.

Assemble the sandwiches by placing one slice of turkey on one slice of bread, a slice of ham on another, then sandwich them with the Swiss cheese in the middle. Secure the sandwich with toothpicks. Preheat oven to 400°F.

Set the nonstick pan over medium heat, add 1 tablespoon olive oil, then crack the eggs into the pan. Place in the preheated oven and cook until the white is set and the yolk is runny.

Dip each sandwich in the batter so that all sides are coated. Deep-fry in the hot oil until golden brown on all sides. Remove toothpicks and arrange on a plate. Dust with powdered sugar, then add the fried egg just before serving. Sprinkle a tiny bit of Maldon salt over the egg yolk and serve with a ramekin of marionberry preserves.

SUNSHINE TAVERN'S PORK BELLY SANDWICH

(SERVES 2)

For the chile mayonnaise:

1 cup mayonnaise
2 tablespoons sriracha (Thai hot sauce)

For the red wine vinaigrette:

⅔ cup red wine vinegar
2 tablespoons extra-virgin olive oil
2 tablespoons canola oil

1 baguette, about 16 inches long
5 tablespoons chile mayonnaise
4 thin slices of Swedish-style Fontina
4 thick slices of tesa (or bacon), seared
    in a pan and crisped
2 small handfuls of arugula
A few thin slices of red onion
Red wine vinaigrette
Kosher salt
Black pepper

Mix the mayonnaise ingredients completely in a small bowl.

Mix the vinaigrette ingredients completely in a small bowl or tight-fitting jar.

Split baguette in half horizontally. Spread chile mayonnaise along the bottom piece of baguette, and top with cheese to cover the length of bread. Lay hot tesa (or bacon) on top of the cheese at a diagonal to cover as much of the baguette as possible.

In a small bowl toss arugula with red onion and enough red wine vinaigrette to gently coat. Season with salt and pepper. Top with salad and close baguette. Cut in four pieces and serve with potato chips.

Jade Teahouse and Patisserie

2342 Southeast Ankeny Street
(503) 236-4998
www.JadePortland.com
Owner: April Eklund
Chef: Lucy Eklund

Located in the Sellwood neighborhood on the east side of the river, Jade Teahouse and Patisserie is a family-run Vietnamese restaurant that is a home away from home for residents of this cool and quiet part of town. Since it opened in October 2008, the restaurant has become increasingly more popular, and it is in the process of building out and up.

Mother/daughter team Lucy and April Eklund are the reason this place is such a jewel. Lucy, a grandmother, cooks and bakes all of the food. Daughter April runs the business. The elder Eklund had a restaurant in Portland for ten years and decided to retire. Not used to idle time, Lucy traveled to France to study baking. Back home, she was restless, and she and April decided to open a little place where she could make the

SESAME BALL
rispy rice ball filled with
onut & sweet yellow bean
w/ coconut caramel dipping sauce

$1.5

gluten free

food of her country of origin, as well as bake breads and pastries from her schooling in Paris. The baguettes, baked every day, are crusty on the outside and soft and warm on the inside.

The menu is large, with over sixty loose teas and some of the best truffle fries in PDX. The spicy green papaya salad is fiery and sweet, and the homemade rice noodles make for a stand-out udon soup. Lunchtime is busy, with neighborhood people coming in for one of the fantastic sandwiches on the freshly baked baguettes. The fried catfish in a curry sauce pairs beautifully with the spinach and rice, and the Vietnamese beef stew is a perfect dish for bread dunking.

For dessert a personal favorite is the Thai ice tea with the black rice pudding with coconut milk and green tea. The sesame balls filled with bean paste deliver a burst of chewy sweetness, and they sell out daily. The food at Jade is very reasonably priced, and it is nice to be in a place filled with motherly love.

CHICKEN SANDWICH

(MAKES 5 SANDWICHES)

2 pounds boned chicken breasts
1 cup soy sauce
½ cup red wine
¼ cup white sugar
¼ cup honey
1 tablespoon grated fresh ginger
½ tablespoon garlic powder
1 teaspoon black pepper

For the slaw:

½ cup water
¼ cup sugar
¼ cup distilled white vinegar
1 cup julienned carrots
1 cup julienned daikon
Salt to taste

For assembly:

5 small baguettes
5 tablespoons mayonnaise
Chicken slices
5 teaspoons soy sauce
1 cucumber, cut lengthwise
Sprigs of cilantro

Preheat the oven to 350°F. Mix ingredients and marinate overnight. Bake uncovered for 1 hour. Remove from the oven and set aside covered with foil to keep warm.

Combine all of the slaw ingredients. Slice open the baguettes and spread with mayonnaise. Spread with the slaw and then with the sliced chicken.

Drizzle with the soy sauce and top with the cucumber and sprigs of cilantro.

LARGE PLATES

It goes without saying that Portland is a food lover's town. Any meal, any time, there is terrific food to be had that is reasonably priced and prepared by seriously talented and inspired chefs. The mild climate and proximity of farms and ranches allow the people in the kitchen to celebrate the region's bounty with fresh, innovative creations.

There is a plethora of great entree choices, from pan-seared chicken on a bread salad at Roost to the fork-tender lamb shanks at Ya Hala. Portland is a very "porky" town, with many restaurants serving all of the pig, not just a couple of slices of pork tenderloin or a chop. The Whole Hog plate at Country Cat (see page 78) is a good example of this, and there is bacon in and on everything. And the beef is extraordinary, from the deeply flavored and rich marrowbones at the Laurelhurst Market (see page 19) to the delicious and almost naughty Yakuza burger.

There are also extraordinary vegetarian options, like the sunchoke bread pudding with brioche, chanterelles, fennel, and hazelnuts at Natural Selection (see page 12) or the Swiss chard and porcini lasagna from DOC, not to mention Ned Ludd Chef-Owner Jason French's wood oven–cooked vegetables, which could turn the strongest carnivore into a vegetarian. Chefs are respectful and accommodating to the people who are vegan or gluten-free, and there are places that create magic with their treatment of all things vegetable.

The recipes included here give you just some idea of the large (and delicious) plates that can be enjoyed in PDX.

Davis Street Tavern

500 Northwest Davis Street
(503) 505-5050
WWW.DAVISSTREETTAVERN.COM
Owners: Christopher Handford and Blake Smith
Chef: Katy Jane Millard

Cousins Christopher Handford and Blake Smith, both front-of-the-house guys, were truly pioneers when they opened Davis Street Tavern in Portland's Old Town. A neighborhood that was at one time full of warehouses and somewhat questionable clubs and bars, Old Town is now undergoing a huge renaissance, and this fine food-serving tavern is considered a local haunt for the businesspeople who have taken up residence in the new offices.

The restaurant is huge. There is seating for about one hundred people between the front dining room and bar and the back two-leveled dining area and the outdoor tables. The main room is handsome and comfortable, with spacious tables and booths, neutral tones, wood beams, and exposed pipes. This is a restaurant where you always feel welcome and never feel rushed. The restaurant is open for lunch and dinner every

day, and there is always a steady flow of customers leisurely enjoying the simple and pure cooking of Chef Katy Jane Millard, who lived and learned from the best in Paris and the south of France for five years.

Millard is deeply committed to serving food to the PDX community while being conscious of giving back to the people who make it all possible. She forms close relationships with all of her local vendors and sticks to the philosophy that going too far from home to purchase her supplies would be disloyal to her clients.

The Davis Street Tavern menu offers a wide range of choices, from the tasty and spicy fried chickpeas and the Calabrian chile duck wings to the velvety mac and cheese and the outstanding tomatillo-glazed pork ribs. Brunch is done very well, with the hazelnut waffles stealing the show. The halibut dish below is a stunning example of Millard's cooking philosophy.

Halibut with Almond Pesto & Potatoes

(SERVES 4)

2 pounds yellow potatoes
¼ cup olive oil
Salt to taste
1 bunch asparagus
4 6-ounce halibut fillets, skin off
Salt and black pepper to taste
2 tablespoons olive oil
1 sprig of thyme
3 tablespoons unsalted butter
1 pound arugula, washed and dried
¼ cup olive oil
Salt and black pepper to taste
Juice of 2 lemons

For the almond pesto:

1 small clove garlic
Zest of ½ lemon
¼ cup olive oil
Pinch of salt
Juice of 1 lemon
½ cup whole almonds, skin on

Cook the potatoes, with skins on, in boiling salted water until tender but not falling apart. Drain them and let them cool slightly. Peel them while they are still warm, then smash them lightly with the back of a spoon (they should be kind of chunky). Stir in ¼ cup good olive oil and salt to taste, adding more olive oil if the potatoes seem dry. Cover and keep warm.

Snap the bottom woody part off the asparagus and discard. Season the halibut fillets with salt and pepper. Heat 2 tablespoons olive oil in a large sauté pan. When the pan is very hot but not yet smoking, carefully add the halibut and turn down the heat to medium. Cook until nicely browned on one side, turn the fish, and add the thyme, butter, and asparagus to the pan, turning down

the heat if the butter starts to brown quickly. Baste the fish and asparagus with the butter until the fish is almost cooked (the flesh should feel firm but should still give a little in the middle). You can remove the asparagus from the pan if it cooks before the fish is done (this will depend on the size of the asparagus and the thickness of the halibut). Drain on paper towels and keep warm; the fish will finish cooking as it sits.

Make the almond pesto: In a food processor, combine the garlic, zest of half a lemon, ¼ cup olive oil, ¾ of the arugula, a good pinch of salt, the juice of one lemon, and the almonds (on top). Process until pestolike in consistency, adding more oil if necessary. Taste, and adjust the acid and salt; it should be nice and tart.

Assemble the dish: Season the remaining arugula with olive oil, salt, pepper, and lemon juice to taste. Spread about 3 tablespoons of pesto on a plate, top with a generous spoonful of potatoes, as much asparagus as you would like, a lovely piece of halibut, and some arugula salad. Springtime on a plate!

Serrato

2112 Northwest Kearney Street
(503) 221-1195
www.serrato.com
Executive Chef: Tony Meyers

Born in southern California, Executive Chef Tony Meyers grew up in a farm-to-table family. His dad worked in construction but had a love of farming and grew vegetables and raised animals on their three acres of land. Meyers credits his paternal grandma for her southern Italian cooking, having given him an appreciation for fine food and using the freshest ingredients at a young age. He started working in restaurants at sixteen as a dishwasher and moved up the chain to sous chef within a short time. Meyers attended the California Culinary Academy and had a series of jobs in San Francisco and Seattle before settling in Portland. He started as sous chef at Serrato in 2006, and became head chef the next year. Serrato is a comfortable restaurant with a rustic Italian vibe. Whether you are a party of two out on a date or a large bunch of work buddies who want to celebrate in a friendly and chill atmosphere, dining at this popular restaurant is a sure bet.

The pizzas are good, with the toppings always reflecting farm-delivered freshness. Tuna tartar incise is refreshing, light, and full of flavor. There are several excellent entrees, like the seared sea scallops and the duck breast, but if you are looking for something a little heartier and unbelievably tender, the pork chop is everything you hope it will be. The chocolate cobbler is one of my favorite desserts in Portland.

Serrato has a large, lively bar that draws the after-work set to this energetic and elegant neighborhood restaurant serving dishes from Italy, France, and the Mediterranean region, all with a Portland spin. Bartender Kurt Fritzler has been at Serrato for almost thirty years; his cocktails are inventive and impressive, and his charming and upbeat personality has earned him a loyal following. Fritzler is the person to ask if you are looking for some special libation to accompany your meal. He totally has it down, and I have never been disappointed with his suggestions.

Citrus Braised Pork Shoulder with Eggplant Tagine

(SERVES 6–8)

For the Moroccan spice rub:

1 teaspoon cumin
1 teaspoon ground ginger
½ teaspoon cinnamon
½ teaspoon allspice
½ teaspoon clove
Pinch of cayenne

For the pork:

5 pounds boneless pork shoulder
Kosher salt
2 tablespoons olive oil
1 yellow onion, cut into quarters
5 cups orange juice
¾ cup lime juice

2 quarts chicken stock

½ bunch cilantro

2 pods cardamom

1 tablespoon coriander seed

For the eggplant tagine:

2 eggplants, peeled and diced, cut into ½-inch cubes

Salt

2 tablespoons olive oil

1 onion, diced

1 tablespoon chopped garlic

½ cup white wine

1 teaspoon ground coriander

1 teaspoon ground cumin

1 teaspoon ground ginger powder

½ teaspoon sweet smoked paprika

Pinch of saffron

1 (28-ounce) can stewed tomatoes

¼ cup lime juice

8 cups prepared couscous with 1 cup golden raisins

½ cup toasted chopped almonds (for garnish)

Mix the spice rub ingredients together and set aside.

Slice the pork shoulder into 3 slices, salt the pieces, and chill for 6 hours or overnight.

Preheat the oven to 350°F. Rub each piece of pork with the Moroccan spice rub.

In a medium sauté pan with 2 tablespoons of oil on medium-high heat, sear each piece of pork for 1 to 2 minutes on each side until golden brown.

Transfer the pork to a braising pan, add the onion and remaining ingredients to the pan, and bring the dish up to a gentle simmer. Cover with a lid and bake for 3 hours or until tender.

Meanwhile, make the eggplant tagine: Salt the eggplants evenly and let them sit out on a towel to soak out any bitterness for 1 hour. Rinse and dry on paper towels.

In a large saucepot over medium heat, sauté the onions in oil. Add the eggplant and continue cooking and stirring frequently, 3 to 5 minutes.

Add the garlic, stir for another minute, deglaze with white wine, and add spices and tomatoes. Then bring the sauce up to a boil.

Reduce the heat to simmer for about 1½ hours until desired thickness. In the last 15 minutes, add the lime juice.

To plate, serve the pork shoulder over a bed of golden raisins and couscous, spoon the tagine over the pork, add the green beans, and sprinkle chopped almonds across the top.

LITTLE BIRD

219 SOUTHWEST 6TH AVENUE
(503) 688-5952
WWW.LITTLEBIRDBISTRO.COM
CHEF: ERIK VAN KLEY
OWNERS: GABRIEL RUCKER AND ANDY FORTGANG

Little Bird is a cousin, or perhaps sibling, of Gabe Rucker's Le Pigeon (see page 28). Having opened in 2010, it immediately garnered interest from the community, and any chef who has the faith and backing of Chef Rucker is off to a grand start. Little Bird is on the west side of the river, so it tends to draw a more west side crowd from the large concentration there of businesses, galleries, and theaters. The menu is French bistro, and Chef Erik Van Kley is adept at creating exactly what you are longing for in the brasserie repertoire. Van Kley grew up in Michigan. He began working in restaurants at sixteen. The restaurant industry felt like the right fit from the beginning, and he quickly climbed the food ladder, going from dishwasher to sous chef in only four years.

Starters are delicious, particularly the smoked trout *gougères,* which are delicate and taste great with the dressing, flavored with hints of citrus and caraway. I am a sucker for steak tartare, especially when there are plenty of tasty additions, and Van Kley's version does not disappoint. The trout with an almond puree rather than the traditional sliced almonds is grilled perfectly, and the cauliflower crepe with Mornay sauce will make any vegetarian dining companion a happy camper.

The staff is professional and knowledgeable about the food and wines, often providing explanations to those unfamiliar with French food and encouraging them to try something new, explaining with gusto the preparations of some of the classic dishes. The room is bustling with a different energy than many other PDX spots, which often tend to be quite low-key. Little Bird, by contrast, feels Parisian and kind of special: festive and a good place to go for a celebration.

Though the menu is French in style and sensibility, the Northwest products dictate what is on the menu based on the season and availability of only the freshest ingredients. It is a no-brainer that Little Bird would fly high under the wing of Le Pigeon.

GRILLED FLAT IRON STEAKS WITH TOMATO SALAD, SPICY REMOULADE & ESPELETTE OIL

(SERVES 6)

For the remoulade sauce:

Juice of 1 lemon
⅛ cup whole grain mustard
⅛ cup yellow mustard
⅛ cup prepared horseradish
1 tablespoon Worcestershire sauce
½ tablespoon Tabasco
3 garlic cloves, chopped
3 scallions, chopped
2 egg yolks
1½ stalks of celery, chopped
1 tablespoon paprika
½ teaspoon cayenne
¾ cup blended oil (two parts canola, one part olive oil)

For the steak marinade:

Leaves from one head of celery, chopped
2 cups chopped whole leaf parsley
1 bunch green onions, chopped
2 garlic cloves, chopped
1 teaspoon salt
About 1 cup blended oil (three parts canola,
    one part olive oil)

For the Espelette oil:

¼ cup dried, ground Espelette pepper
    (French chile pepper)
1 cup blended oil (half olive, half canola)
6 flat iron steaks, about 6–7 ounces each
Salt and black pepper to taste

For the tomato salad:

Assorted cherry tomatoes, grape tomatoes, and
    teardrop tomatoes, cut in half, about 1 cup
    per person
Red onion rounds, shaved paper thin
Pickled garlic, shaved paper thin
Picked whole leaf parsley, 4–5 leaves per person
2–3 tablespoons extra-virgin olive oil
2 tablespoons lemon juice
Salt to taste

Prepare the remoulade sauce: In a food
processor, add all remoulade sauce ingredients
except the oil; blend until well combined. With
the processor running, slowly add the oil. Adjust
the seasoning with salt, pepper, and a little more
lemon juice.

Remoulade sauce may be prepared several days
in advance. Allow it to chill in the refrigerator.

Prepare the steak marinade: Place all
ingredients in a food processor and process to a
pestolike consistency.

Prepare the Espelette oil: Place both
ingredients in a small saucepan and bring to a
very gentle simmer, store overnight, then strain
and reserve oil.

Day-of preparation and assembly: Rub steaks with the marinade and let sit for at least 1 hour. Season steaks with salt and pepper and grill or broil to desired temperature; let rest about 2 minutes before slicing.

While the steaks are on the grill, prepare the tomato salad. Dress the assorted tomatoes with fresh red onions, sliced pickled garlic, whole leaf parsley, olive oil, lemon juice, and salt to taste.

Arrange tomato salads on 6 plates and top with the grilled, sliced steak. Spoon the remoulade over the steaks, drizzle the Espelette oil around the plate, and serve.

Bar Mingo

811 Northwest 21st Avenue
(503) 445-4646
www.barmingonw.com
Owner: Michael Cronin
Chef: Jerry Huisinga

Bar Mingo, a softly hued bar/restaurant, was developed for two—actually three—reasons. First, the space became available, and it was impossible to pass up for owner Michael Cronin, who has the very successful Caffe Mingo next door. Second, it would be a place for the Caffe Mingo diners to have a comfortable spot to have fabulous cocktails and wines while waiting for their table next door. Third, Cronin wanted a place that would function as a bar as much as a restaurant, a place to drink and dine with smaller portions and prices, perfect for tasting and sharing.

Bar Mingo is small—ten tables, twelve seats at the bar, and a super-comfortable seating area with sofas and cocktail tables. There is rotating art on the walls and a giant chalk board with a huge drawing of the map of Italy, hand-drawn by the clearly multitalented chef, Jerry Huisinga.

Huisinga is one of the finest chefs cooking Italian food in PDX today. He has been cooking in town for some thirty years, twenty-two of them at Genoa, a restaurant that, in its heyday, was at the forefront of Portland's changing food scene. After leaving Genoa, Huisinga came to work at Caffe Mingo, where he continued to create inspired Italian food in anticipation of the opening of Bar Mingo. He is an advocate of simple, seasonal, full-flavored food that is not disguised with heavy sauces. Huisinga has a strong following and the respect of the Portland food community.

LAMB MEATBALLS IN TOMATO SAUCE
FLAVORED WITH OREGANO & MINT

(SERVES 8)

⅔ cup milk

2 slices hearty bread, crusts removed

2 pounds ground lamb

¼ cup finely chopped onion

2 tablespoons finely chopped Italian parsley

¼ teaspoon grated nutmeg

2 eggs

⅓ cup grated Parmesan cheese

2 tablespoons olive oil

Salt and pepper to taste

Dry bread crumbs for coating the meatballs

For the sauce:

6 tablespoons olive oil (reserve 3 tablespoons
    for frying meatballs)

1 onion, chopped

3 cloves garlic, chopped

¼ cup chopped fresh mint

1 tablespoon dried oregano

½ cup white wine

2 (28-ounce) cans whole tomatoes

¼ cup roughly chopped mint

For the garnish:

¼ cup roughly chopped Italian parsley

½ cup ground pecorino Romano cheese

Put the milk and bread into a saucepan and bring to a boil. Mash the bread with a fork and blend it uniformly into the milk. Set aside and let cool before proceeding with the next step.

In a mixing bowl put the ground lamb, onion, parsley, nutmeg, eggs, Parmesan cheese, oil, the bread and milk mixture, and salt and pepper to taste. Mix everything thoroughly but gently by hand.

Gently, without squeezing, shape the mixture into small round balls about 1½ inches in diameter. Roll the meatballs in the dry bread crumbs to coat. Refrigerate while making the sauce.

In a heavy bottomed pot, heat 3 tablespoons olive oil until hot. Add the chopped onions and garlic and sauté until beginning to soften. Add the fresh mint and dry oregano. Add the wine and continue to cook until the wine has all but disappeared. Add the canned tomatoes and bring to a boil. Lower to a simmer and cook sauce until it is thickened. You may want to put the sauce through a food mill if you want it smoother.

Meanwhile, preheat the oven to 400°F. Heat 3 tablespoons olive oil in a frying pan over medium heat until hot. Add the meatballs and fry, turning to brown on all sides. You may have to do this in batches. Take care not to crowd the meatballs. Keep meatballs warm until all of them are browned. Place the meatballs into an ovenproof casserole with as much sauce as you need to cover the balls halfway. Place in the preheated oven for about 10 minutes to finish cooking.

To serve, dust liberally with grated pecorino Romano cheese and sprinkle with chopped fresh mint and oregano.

CAFFE MINGO

807 Northwest 21st Avenue
(503) 226-4646
WWW.CAFFEMINGONW.COM
Owner: Michael Cronin
Chef: Brett West

Caffe Mingo serves some of the best Italian food in town. The restaurant, located in northwestern Portland, was serving rustic authentic cuisine well before the PDX food scene exploded. Michael Cronin, the owner of Caffe Mingo and its next door neighbor, Bar Mingo, was at the forefront of the farm-to-table movement, serving simple and local reasonably priced food in a casual atmosphere and an Italian venue. Cronin came to Portland to visit a friend in 1975 and never left. The restaurant began with a pizza by the slice concept, and over the first few years the specials offered in addition to the pizza began to gain popularity. It morphed into a more sophisticated restaurant while still maintaining its casual vibe.

Caffe Mingo is small, seating about forty people at the wooden tables and bar for both drinking and dining. The open kitchen, which for years operated with nothing more than a pizza oven, has been upgraded to include a hood and a grill. The restaurant has the feel of a cafe in Italy, and the always perfect tomatoes, fabulous bread, and small but well-selected wine list add to the authentic Italian atmosphere. It is not unusual to wait for a table at Caffe Mingo. Much to his steady customers' dismay, Cronin wants to keep the seating this way. Besides, the wait is never very long, and it is always worth it.

Chef Brett West has been with Cronin for over seven years. The menu is a tribute to Italian comfort food, with everything made from scratch and only the freshest products. The pizzas are thin-crust marvels of the finest ingredients, the pastas handmade and extraordinary. Just about all the items on the menu are winners, and from your first bite of the amazing crusty bread and olive oil to the velvety panna cotta, you will leave a most satisfied customer.

PENNE AL SUGO DI CARNE

(SERVES 6)

3 pounds beef bottom round, trimmed of fat and sliced into 2-inch strips (cut across the grain, not with the grain)

Salt and pepper to taste

4 tablespoons Unsalted butter

4 tablespoons extra virgin olive oil oil

1 red onion, peeled and sliced

1½ cups Chianti wine (not "cooking" wine, something you would drink)

16 ounces canned stewed tomatoes

16 ounces tomato puree

½ cup espresso

1½ pounds pasta (penne is good)

1 tablespoon unsalted butter

1 cup stock (beef, chicken, or vegetable)

Salt and black pepper to taste

Preheat the oven to 400°F. Season the sliced beef with salt and pepper. In a large heavy bottomed pan, heat butter on medium-high heat. Sear the beef in butter and add onions. Cook on medium until onions are tender. Add red wine, tomatoes, tomato puree, and espresso.

Cover and place in the oven for 1 to 2 hours or until the meat is very tender and easily pulls apart. Remove the beef from the sauce and shred. Puree the sauce or put it through a food mill. Add the shredded beef back to the pureed sauce and refrigerate.

Bring a large pot of water to a rolling boil. Add some coarse salt. Cook the pasta until done, according to the package directions.

To serve: Place 2 cups of the meat sauce in a sauté pan with butter and stock. On medium heat, bring to a simmer, season to taste with salt and pepper, and toss with your favorite, just cooked pasta.

Pok Pok

3226 Southeast Division Street
(503) 232-1387
www.pokpokpdx.com

1469 Northeast Prescott Street
(503) 287-4149
www.pokpoknoi.com
Chef and Owner: Andy Ricker

Just about everyone who has come to visit us in PDX has Pok Pok on his or her to-do list. Vermont-born Chef Andy Ricker has achieved national (perhaps international) notoriety for his spicy, at times fiery, Thai street food. Having spent years traveling through Thailand, meeting and eating and learning, Ricker opened a shack on the then essentially undeveloped Division Street. Word spread fast, and before long there were lines of people waiting to eat the famous chicken wings and the tender and flavorful Cornish hen. Both dishes are memorable, and it is not surprising that once the word got out, Pok Pok received a ton of press, numerous awards, and a thriving business. A couple of other not-to-be-missed dishes are the Naua Naam Tok, a spicy-hot steak salad made with fish sauce, lemongrass, mint, and cilantro, and the Cha Ca "la Vong," which is a Vietnamese catfish dish flavored with turmeric, green onions, and dill, served on a bed of rice vermicelli with chopped peanuts and cilantro.

The menu at Pok Pok is unusual, offering many dishes that have only been on menus or in carts on the streets of Thailand.

It is common knowledge that unless it is an off hour, there will be some waiting time at Pok Pok. Ricker made the wait much more pleasant when he opened The Whiskey Soda Lounge in 2010. The cocktails are great, and the snacks, a little offbeat and unusual, have turned the waiting experience into a two-part dining adventure.

Not too long ago, Ricker opened another eatery, Pok Pok Noi, a small takeout and counter dining spot with a menu of about twelve dishes, happily including the famous ribs and Cornish hen.

YAM MUU KROB

CRISPY PORK BELLY SALAD

(SERVES 2)

For this dish, go to your friendly local Chinese barbecue joint and buy ½ pound crispy roasted pork. Tell them you want the belly part.

For the dressing:

1 ½ ounces lime juice

1 ounce fish sauce

1 ½ ounces palm sugar syrup*

2 tablespoon garlic, thinly sliced

2 teaspoons Thai chilies, chopped

8 ounces muu krob (crispy pork belly),
    sliced into ¼ x 1-inch pieces

1 cup thinly sliced white onion

4 tablespoons roughly chopped Chinese celery

2 tablespoons chopped green onion

16 cherry tomatoes, halved

4 tablespoons torn cilantro

Mix equal parts palm sugar and hot water; stir to make syrup.

Prepare the dressing: In a small saucepan, heat the dressing ingredients until just warm.

In a medium mixing bowl, combine the pork, white onion, Chinese celery, chopped scallions, and the cherry tomatoes. Add the dressing, toss, and turn out onto plates. Top with cilantro.

Ned Ludd

3925 Northeast Martin Luther King Junior Boulevard
(503) 288-6900
WWW.NEDLUDDPDX.COM
Chef and Owner: Jason French

Ned Ludd, which opened its doors in 2008, is in a category of its own. All the cooking in the restaurant is done in the wood-burning oven, which is just about the only thing left in the building from its days as a pizza place, long before the farm-to-table movement hit its stride. The room is cozy and inviting and has the feeling of a cabin or a shed that has been transformed into a unique place to get simple food that reflects the season's offerings. (The name, by the way, comes from the folkloric founder of the Luddite movement, a reaction to the growing reliance on machines during the industrial revolution in England.)

The food takes advantage of what the region has to offer, and the results are the expression of the combinations of the products and the magic of the wood-stoked oven.

Chef-Owner Jason French could very well be the spokesman for the American craft kitchen movement, talking with great enthusiasm about community and keeping things fresh and completely local. French wants his restaurant to move as far away from big business and mass food production as can be achieved. Talking with him is inspirational because he feels so committed to taking care of what the earth has to offer, and also the people who work to make it all happen.

The baked-to-order flatbread, with a sprinkling of seasonal herbs and spices, is a great place to start, along with some house-brined pickles or olives. There is always an extravagant charcuterie plate and unusual, and of course local, cheeses, as well as a meat pie—I've never had one that was a disappointment. The kitchen is masterful with vegetables; on a recent visit, the butter lettuce with smoked trout and lemon cream was magic.

The large plates change frequently, and they're consistently wonderful. A smoked cod with mussels and horseradish is phenomenal, as is the pork and beans, oven-roasted with just-picked greens. I love the duck breast with the mashed rutabaga redolent with earthy flavors. The stuffed ruby trout is perfumed with fennel and citrus, and it is a perfect dish to show off the magic of the oven.

Stuffed Ruby Trout, Fennel, Scallion, Lemon & Herbs

(SERVES 4)

4 whole ruby trout, deboned (steelhead or rainbow also acceptable)

Sea salt to taste

1 teaspoon ground fennel seed

½ teaspoon ground white pepper

½ teaspoon ground brown mustard seed

½ teaspoon ground yellow mustard seed

2 lemons, halved lengthwise and thinly sliced

2 fennel bulbs, halved, cored, and thinly sliced, plus fronds

2 bunches green onion, trimmed and halved through the stalk

2 lemons, halved, for juicing

2 radishes, thinly sliced

½ cup flat leaf parsley, stemmed and chopped

2 tablespoons tarragon, stemmed and roughly chopped

2 tablespoons chives

Extra-virgin olive oil (to finish)

Preheat the oven to 500°F. Place the rack on the lowest level. Open the trout to expose the flesh. Season with salt and spices. Place lemon and fennel fronds evenly over the flesh and fold the fish over. Lightly oil and season the fish on both sides.

Scatter the fennel and scallion over a sheet pan or a large cast iron skillet. Place the trout on the pan. Roast fish for 6 to 8 minutes. Set the broiler on high and move the fish to the highest level. Move the fish under the broiler and roast another 5 to 7 minutes until the skin is crisp and the vegetables are browned.

Place the fish on individual plates. Scatter the vegetables over the fish. Squeeze half a lemon over each fish. Finish with radishes, herbs, extra-virgin olive oil, and sea salt. Serve immediately.

Roost

1403 SOUTHEAST BELMONT STREET
(971) 544-7136
WWW.ROOSTPDX.COM
CHEF AND OWNER: MEGAN HENZEL

For those who yearn for food and drink that's simple and without pretension, Roost may just be the perfect place. Opened in 2010 by Chef and Owner Megan Henzel, this restaurant strives to make the diners feel more like guests in someone's home rather than patrons. Roost is on Belmont Street, on the heavily hipstered east side of Portland.

Henzel is always working the line, but if you get a chance to talk with her, it is clear that she is as passionate about her cooking as Portland is about eating. She is just lovely. An Oregon native, she grew up in Klamath Falls. She headed east and attended cooking school in Cambridge, Massachusetts, then worked her way around some of Boston's finest restaurants, including a stint with Gordon Hamersley. Megan studied the works of M. F. K. Fisher and actually had the honor of working in the kitchen with Julia Child on a couple of occasions.

After her time in Boston, Henzel headed to New York, where she cooked in some notable restaurants before working as a private chef in the ultra-chic and over-the-top

wealthy Hamptons, on the South Shore of Long Island. Henzel spent three years serving food on $5,000 plates and having her clients arrive at the house for the weekend in their private helicopters. It was a great learning experience, but it left her with a desire for a much simpler and far less pretentious life.

By this time Henzel's family had moved to Portland, and that, combined with the exploding food scene, made moving to PDX a no-brainer. She looked at property and found a corner spot in a welcoming neighborhood that would lend itself to the kind of food she likes to cook.

The Roost menu is small, but there are always enough tempting things to make the decision a challenge. The deep-fried pork ribs with blue cheese butter, house-made barbecue sauce, and black-eyed peas far exceed my already high expectations, and the shredded radicchio with fried goat cheese, black olives, and crisp bacon is up there with the all-time best salads.

SEARED PANZANELLA CHICKEN

(SERVES 4)

1 cup olive oil

12 garlic cloves, peeled

4 boneless chicken breasts

4 boneless chicken thighs

16 good-size chunks day-old bread,
    drizzled with olive oil and coarse salt

⅓ cup pitted oil-cured black olives

4 cups chicken stock

Salt and black pepper to taste

¼ cup chopped parsley

For the salad:

1 bunch arugula, cleaned and dried on
    a clean dish towel

¼ cup sherry vinegar

¾ cup olive oil

1 tablespoon sugar

Preheat the oven to 450°F. In a small pan, add one cup of olive oil and 12 cloves of garlic. Slowly caramelize the garlic until tender. In a skillet, pan sear the chicken pieces and place on a baking sheet until all pieces are seared. Place in the preheated oven to roast. Cut up chunks of day-old bread and drizzle with olive oil and salt (about four cubes of bread per person). Place in oven to toast.

Once chicken is cooked through, remove from the pan and keep warm. Discard oil from the pan and add pitted olives, the garlic, and chicken stock. Scrape the bottom of the pan to get all the crust. Taste, then add salt and pepper and chopped parsley. Remove toasted bread and place on plates. Spoon the sauce over the warm croutons. Top with the arugula salad dressed with sherry vinegar, olive oil, and sugar and warm roasted chicken.

RICOTTA

After swooning over the starter house-made ricotta with smashed peas, I needed more info. Megan Henzel, who cooks wonderful and completely unpretentious food as the chef and owner of Roost, offered her easy and super tasty ricotta recipe, along with several recipes that incorporate this creamy treat. I will never buy ricotta again.

6 cups milk
2 cups heavy cream
3 cups buttermilk

Mix all the ingredients in a pot and stir, bring to a simmer and allow the curds to form. Do not let it come to a full boil. You will see the curds floating up to the surface. 10-15 minutes is all it takes. Strain thru a chinois or cheesecloth.

SMASHED PEAS ON BREAD

4 slices good quality bread, toasted
⅔ cup ricotta
½ cup cooked peas, gently smashed
Extra-virgin olive oil
Coarse black pepper
Salt

Place the toasted bread on your work surface. Lightly spread the ricotta on each slice of bread.

Divide the peas and place on each bread slice.

Drizzle with olive oil and sprinkle with salt and pepper.

RICOTTA PANCAKES

1½ cups all-purpose flour
2 large eggs
½ cup buttermilk
⅓ cup ricotta
2 tablespoons sugar
1 teaspoon baking soda
½ teaspoon salt

Mix all ingredients together. Prepare as you would your old favorite pancake recipe. This will be your new fave. Serve with maple syrup.

RICOTTA & FRESH FRUIT

2 cups ricotta cheese
3 tablespoons honey
½ teaspoon vanilla extract
Finely grated zest of 1 small orange
2–3 drops pure almond extract
2 cups assorted fresh fruit cut in bite-size pieces
½ cup raspberries pureed with 2 teaspoons sugar

In a medium bowl combine the ricotta, honey, vanilla, orange zest, and the almond extract.

Divide among four bowls. Top with the mixed fruit and then with the pureed berries.

GILT CLUB

306 NORTHWEST BROADWAY
(503) 222-4458
WWW.GILTCLUB.COM
EXECUTIVE CHEF: CHRIS CARRIKER
OWNER: JAMIE DUNN

After hearing rave reviews about the sold-out Plate and Pitchfork dinner with Gilt Club chef Chris Carriker, I realized I must be missing something special. Plate and Pitchfork is a series of dinners at farms throughout the area, planned with the intention of raising awareness of sustainable farming. Additionally, some of the dinners' proceeds go to organizations that support small farms. After hearing several local chefs mention that Gilt Club is their favorite late-night restaurant, both for food and drink, my husband and I made a reservation.

Chef Carriker was raised in Washington State, worked in kitchens during his high school years, and did some time studying at the Western Culinary Institute. He worked at some of Portland's best restaurants, including 23 Hoyt, before being offered his current gig at Gilt Club. He is friendly with a delightful sense of humor and just seems to love what he does. It is not unusual to see him zipping around town on his super-cool Vespa.

Our recent dinner at Gilt Club confirmed the reports. The menu was full of foods calling out to me. The fries, which I am always unable to pass up, are cooked in duck fat and topped with Parmesan, herbs, and a roasted garlic aioli. What a great way to start a meal! The chicken liver mousse is the best I have had here in Portland, served on crusty toast and a cipollini onion agrodolce (a traditional sweet-and-sour sauce in Italian cuisine).

The polenta topped with a poached duck egg and served with duck bacon and an herbed salsa is also first rate; the polenta has the perfect texture and is a great contrast to the crisp bacon and the just-fried pork cracklin. Carriker makes a mean saddle of rabbit, and his roasted pheasant with figs gets high marks as well.

We topped off this amazing meal with a chocolate dessert, a trio of hazelnut bark, warm chocolate cake, and chocolate mousse with a little salt and pepper, all sitting so happily on a bed of Nutella, the totally rad chocolate hazelnut spread. I left thinking that I didn't have room for another bite, and I wasn't sure if I should feel proud or embarrassed that we ate the whole thing.

BRAISED SHORT RIBS

(SERVES 6)

For the short ribs:

5 sprigs of fresh thyme

4 cloves of garlic, thinly sliced

1 sprig of rosemary, finely chopped

4 tablespoons finely chopped parsley

Salt and pepper to taste

4 tablespoons olive oil

6 2-inch-cut short ribs

1 medium yellow onion, medium dice

2 stalks of celery, sliced

2 medium carrots, sliced

1 bottle of red wine (Cabernet or Syrah would be nice)

3 cups veal stock

For the black vinegar sauce:

Splash of olive oil

2 shallots, finely sliced

2 cloves garlic, smashed

1 sprig of fresh thyme

1 (5-ounce) bottle of black vinegar
    (can be found at local Asian markets)

½ cup packed brown sugar

Zest of 1 orange

1 Thai chile (optional)

2 cups braising liquid from the short ribs

Salt and pepper to taste

For the charred eggplant:

1 large eggplant

¼ cup extra-virgin olive oil

Lemon juice

Salt and pepper to taste

½ cup peanuts, fried and chopped (for garnish)

Preheat the oven to 350°F. In a deep-sided dish large enough to hold the ribs, mix the thyme, garlic, rosemary, parsley, salt, pepper, and olive oil, and add the ribs, covering well. Marinate the ribs for at least 3 hours to overnight.

In a large pan heat the oil to moderate-high, then brown the ribs on each side until a crust develops (it takes about 10 minutes). Transfer ribs to a braising dish.

In the large pan add the onions, celery, and carrots; cook until soft and slightly caramelized. Once caramelized, add to short ribs. Then carefully deglaze the pan with the red wine. (To avoid any possibility of burning yourself, it's best to remove the pan from the stovetop before adding the wine.)

Once the wine has loosened the stuck-on particles from the pan and has reduced by a third, strain and add to the short ribs. Cover the short ribs and vegetables with the veal stock.

Bring everything to a high simmer, then cover and cook for about 2½ hours or until the meat is fork tender.

While the meat is braising, use a little oil to slightly caramelize the shallots, garlic, and thyme together. Then add the black vinegar, brown sugar, orange zest, and if you want a little kick, Thai chile.

Reduce the liquid by half, then strain.

Once the ribs are done, strain the liquid. Try to remove as much fat as possible. Add the braising liquid to the black vinegar reduction and reduce again until the sauce has thickened.

If you have a gas range, simply rub the eggplant with olive oil, salt, and pepper and char on an open burner until black. If you don't have a gas range, rub the eggplant the same way and charbroil in an oven at 500°F, but be sure to turn the eggplant to get even charring.

Once cooled, cut off the top of the eggplant; place the remaining eggplant into a blender with olive oil and blend until smooth. Adjust flavor with a little lemon juice, salt, and pepper.

To finish, put the short ribs in a clean pan, add the black vinegar sauce, and cook together until glazed.

Put charred eggplant as the base on a plate, place short ribs on top, and drizzle black vinegar sauce on and around. Garnish with fried peanuts. You can serve with crusty bread, snow peas, baby carrots, or any other seasonal vegetables.

EAT: An Oyster Bar

3808 North Williams Street
(503) 281-1222
info@eatoystersbar.com
Chef: Ethan Powell
Owners: Tobias Hogan and Ethan Powell

Portland has no shortage of chill, homey restaurants serving good food at an affordable price. EAT fits the bill, but it also has the distinction of being the only oyster bar in town. And the oysters are spectacular. There are often between ten and fifteen varieties, with 75 percent of them coming from the West Coast. The oysters are served on crushed ice, with a couple wedges of lemon, shucked to order, and when they arrive at your table you know they couldn't be fresher. When they are fried, they are crisp and creamy and terrific. The friendly staff really knows their oysters, too.

Chef Ethan Powell, originally from Arkansas, moved to Portland from New York and worked around town cooking in some terrific places, such as Andina (see page 25). When he was settled into Portland life, he started missing the kind of food, and the kind of places, he enjoyed back home.

What Ethan wanted to create with EAT was the feeling of eating in the South in the 1950s before foods were processed and when everything was made from scratch. Nothing was frozen, and the only things not eaten fresh had been canned in someone's kitchen.

The homemade recipes are classics; the étouffées and the gumbos are rich and spicy. To wash them down, there's good beer, traditional Southern sweetened ice tea, and a fine selection of whiskeys, especially in the bourbon category.

Chicken Jambalaya with Andouille

1 (3½-pound) whole farm chicken, quartered

2 tablespoons kosher salt, split

1 tablespoon fresh ground black pepper

2 tablespoons canola oil

3 andouille sausage, sliced in rounds
    about ¼-inch thick

1½ cups diced yellow onion

¾ cup diced celery

¾ cup diced green bell pepper

2 tablespoons minced garlic

1½ teaspoons Santaka chile flakes

3 cups long-grain white rice

6 cups chicken stock

1¼ cups green onion, chopped, green part only
    ¼ cup reserved

Season the chicken pieces with 1 tablespoon each of salt and pepper. Heat the oil in a large casserole with a tight-fitting lid.

Over medium-high heat, sear the chicken quarters until golden brown on both sides.

Once seared, remove the chicken and put quarters on a sheet pan. Add the sliced andouille to the pan and sear, rendering some of the fat. Once crispy, remove the andouille and add it to the chicken.

Remove all but 2 tablespoons of fat from the pan and be careful not to burn any remaining bits. Sauté onion, celery, and green pepper in the pan until soft; add the garlic and chile flakes, and sauté until fragrant. Add the rice and stir until coated with oil and slightly translucent at the ends.

Once the rice has reached the translucent stage, add the chicken stock and remaining salt, stir so there are no clumps of rice, then return the chicken and andouille to the pan, along with 1 cup of the scallions. Bring to a simmer, allowing the

rice to absorb the liquid (it's very important not to stir the jambalaya at this point). Once the liquid is absorbed, remove from heat, cover, and let stand for 10 to 15 minutes.

Remove chicken meat from the bone and chop roughly; gently stir the meat into the finished jambalaya and plate family style or plate using individual bowls. Garnish with remaining scallions.

Paley's Place

1204 Northwest 21st Avenue
(503) 243-2403
www.paleysplace.net
Executive Chef-Owner: Vitaly Paley
General Manager and Owner: Kimberly Paley
Chef de Cuisine: Patrick McKee

Iron Chef winner Vitaly Paley has been running his charming restaurant in an old Victorian house in northwestern Portland since 1995. The restaurant has about fifty seats and is sophisticated in its professionalism and cuisine while remaining friendly and warm. You can eat in the somewhat formal dining rooms, on the front porch, or on the open-air patio; you can also choose to eat at the bar when you are looking for a quick and terrific meal.

The dining rooms at Paley's have a very different feel than almost any other restaurant in town. Paley's may be one of the only places where you would not want to be wearing shorts and a pair of Keens. It's more formal here, although not stuffy; there's an unwritten rule to dress nicely and maybe cover up some of your tattoos.

Paley creates his menu based solely on the bounty of the Pacific Northwest. The escargot Bordelaise with marrow and garlic is outstanding, as is the crispy sweetbreads served with herb spaetzle and mushrooms in a morel cream sauce. The cocktails are done well—my first lemon drop experience was there, and I have been a fan ever since.

Vitaly Paley is partly responsible for the success of many of the PDX stars making food news today. He is generous with his vast knowledge and takes great pride in the accomplishments of those he has mentored. Many of the chefs in this book mention Paley's as their desired place to eat. The restaurant and the food are a treat for all the senses, and one can linger for hours in the tranquil, elegant setting.

Dungeness Crab & Corn Risotto

(SERVES 4–6)

3–4 cups corn broth

¼ cup extra-virgin olive oil

1 small onion, finely diced

Kosher salt and freshly ground black pepper to taste

1⅓ cups carnaroli rice

1 cup dry white wine

6 tablespoons unsalted butter

2 small ears of corn, shucked

1 cup Dungeness crabmeat, drained and picked clean

¾ cup grated Parmesan cheese

¼ cup loosely packed basil leaves,
    cut in chiffonade (thin strips)

¼ cup basil pesto

For the corn broth: (Makes 8 cups)

4 quarts water

8 ears of corn, shucked

2 tablespoons salt

For the basil pesto: (Makes about 1 cup)

¼ cup raw hazelnuts

2 cups fresh basil leaves

3 garlic cloves, coarsely chopped

Juice of half a lemon

¼ cup grated Parmesan cheese

Kosher salt and freshly ground black pepper to taste

½ cup extra-virgin olive oil

Prepare the risotto: In a saucepan bring the broth to a boil over high heat, decrease the heat to low, and keep hot.

In a 3-quart saucepan, warm the olive oil over medium heat. Add the diced onion, season with salt and pepper, and cook without letting the onion color until the pieces are translucent, about 3 minutes. Add the rice all at once, stir to coat with oil, and cook, stirring frequently, about 2 minutes.

Increase the heat to high, add the wine, and continue to cook, stirring gently, until all the wine has been absorbed, about 3 minutes.

Pour in 3 cups of the hot broth and boil for about 10 minutes. Stir occasionally to prevent the rice from sticking to the bottom of the pan. (Don't leave the spoon in the pan between stirrings, or the rice will not cook evenly.)

In a small skillet, melt 4 tablespoons of the butter over low heat. Add the shucked corn and the crab and warm gently for about 5 minutes.

After the rice has cooked for 10 minutes, test for doneness by tasting a few grains. When ready, the center of the grain should still have a little resistance, and the risotto should be fairly liquid. If the rice seems too chewy, cook for another minute. Add the corn-crab mixture to the rice, stirring gently to distribute, and cook another 2 minutes. When ready to serve, the risotto should be the consistency of porridge. If it seems too dry, thin as needed with more broth.

Remove the pan from the heat. Add the remaining 2 tablespoons of butter, along with ½ cup of the grated cheese, and stir the risotto vigorously with one hand while shaking the pot with the other for about 1 minute. The texture will become creamy, and the butter and cheese will be completely incorporated. Stir in the pesto.

Serve in individual bowls, garnished with basil and the remaining ¼ cup Parmesan.

To make the corn broth: In a large pot bring the water to a boil over high heat, add the corn and salt, and cook 5 minutes. Remove the corn and let cool. Using a paring knife, slice off the kernels from the cobs, letting them drop into a bowl. Set the kernels aside if using them right away for another recipe, or refrigerate them in a covered container for no longer than 2 days. You can also freeze them for about 2 weeks.

Halve the 8 stripped cobs crosswise and return them to the pot of cooking water. Simmer over medium-low heat until the broth develops a definite corn flavor, about 45 minutes. Strain the broth, discarding the cobs, and reserve if using right away, or let cool and refrigerate in a covered container. It will keep, refrigerated, for up to 3 days, or frozen for up to 1 month.

To make the basil pesto: In a small skillet, cook the hazelnuts over medium heat, moving the pan back and forth to roll the nuts until they are evenly colored, about 5 minutes. Watch carefully, as they quickly turn brown, then blacken. When the skins start to peel and the nuts give off a toasty aroma, transfer them to a kitchen towel and let cool slightly. Rub them in the towel to get rid of as much papery skin as possible.

In the work bowl of a food processor fitted with the metal blade, add the basil, garlic, hazelnuts, lemon juice, and Parmesan and pulse until coarsely chopped. Season with salt and pepper. Pour in all the olive oil and process until smooth. Refrigerate, covered, until ready to use.

GRÜNER

527 SOUTHWEST 12TH AVENUE
(503) 241-7163
WWW.GRUNERPDX.COM
CHEF AND OWNER: CHRIS ISRAEL

"Change is good" was the answer to the "What's your food philosophy?" question I posed to Chef Chris Israel. This Portland icon is one of the first people who had an impact on the food scene in town, with the opening of the game-changing restaurant Zefero, along with partners Bruce Carey and Monique Siu. Grüner, which means "greener" in German, celebrates the bounty of the Pacific Northwest, expressed through an interesting spin on German food. Just a couple of years old now, Chef Israel's restaurant has quickly captured a loyal following and a fine reputation. The interior is decorated in tones of browns and grays and has a more sophisticated feel than many local haunts.

Israel has had a career that reflects his "change is good" outlook. After having success in the PDX food scene for years, Israel left Portland and had an eight-year stint as the art director of *Vanity Fair* magazine. Israel enjoyed his coveted position at Condé Nast collaborating with writers and photographers, then spent weekends cooking at his cabin in upstate New York. With the draw of friends and family and the lure of the ever-expanding Portland food culture, he came back to town. Here, Israel first worked at a couple of Bruce Carey spots until he opened Grüner in 2009.

The food at Grüner is German, but with a lighter hand. There are fresh and creatively prepared greens and vegetables, and the entrees are not swimming in cream sauce and sauerkraut. The liptauer cheese—a smooth, creamy blend of soft cheeses, capers,

paprika, caraway seeds, and mustard, and served with crackers and assorted crudités— is a light starter and not that easy to find in restaurants. The mushroom-stuffed ravioli is made in-house and is earthy and satisfying, as is the duck breast schnitzel served with a dilled cucumber salad and a Bing cherry-rhubarb sauce. I love duck just about any way it is served, and this preparation is unusual and delectable.

DUCK SCHNITZEL

(SERVES 4)

4 Pekin (Long Island) duck breasts, skin removed

Salt and pepper to taste

1 cup flour

1 large egg, beaten

4 cups panko breadcrumbs, ground fine in a spice grinder

Canola oil

Clean duck breasts, removing center vein from flesh with a paring knife. Cut in half, ideally on a bias. Pound and flatten pieces ¼- to ⅜-inch thick. Season breasts with salt & pepper and dip in flour, shaking off excess. Dip them into beaten egg then into the finely ground panko crumbs.

Into your largest stainless sauté pan pour 1 inch canola oil. Heat over medium-high flame until hot (just rippling). Cook in two four-piece batches; avoid overcrowding the pan. Keep shaking the pan lightly and carefully, continuously rolling hot oil over duck, basting until golden brown. Stay close as they will brown quickly. Turn over and baste the other side.

Remove to paper towels and repeat with remaining breasts.

Hold in a 200°F oven.

RHUBARB-CRANBERRY RELISH

(SERVES 16)

1 cup sugar

1 cup water

Zest from lemon and orange

1 tablespoon grated ginger

1 bag fresh or frozen cranberries

1 pound rhubarb, cut into ½-inch dice, yielding
   approximately 2 cups

Combine sugar, water, zest, and ginger in
a stainless saucepan. Bring to a boil. Add
cranberries and cook until done or until the
berries have popped and barely hold their shape.

Stir in rhubarb and cook just a minute or two
longer. The rhubarb must be cooked through but
not bursting or losing its shape. Remove from
heat. Adjust with more sugar if too tart.

Trader Vic's

1203 Northwest Glisan Street
(503) 467-2277
info@tradervicspdx.com
Chef: Michael Broderick
Owner: Mai Tai Partners

I used to go as a kid to the Polynesian fantasy land that was Trader Vic's on the lower level of the Plaza Hotel in New York City, so I was stoked when I heard that one was coming to town and booked my reservation right away.

We ate in the lounge and ordered Cosmo Tidbits, the original pupu platter, consisting of spareribs, crab Rangoon, crispy prawns, and the sliced pork. I also couldn't resist the duck tacos and the egg rolls, with the crispy skin made in-house. Someone at the next table traded a shrimp for a few Cheese Bings, these yummy panko-crusted treats. The huge wood-fired oven roasts meat, poultry, and seafood to perfection, and all the dishes that come out are smoky with hints of sweetness.

As I agonized about which mai tai to order, the lovely waitress suggested I go for the flight of mai tais, consisting of pineapple, guava, and mango concoctions. I have had flights of wine, beer, scotch, and bourbon and always found them informative and helpful. After my fifth sip of the mai tais, I barely remembered my name, let alone which drink I preferred. They tasted good, sweet, and deceptive, and it made for a fun night. (But be sure to walk here, or have a nondrinker in your party, if you're planning a flight of your own.)

Trader Vic's is filled with original artifacts, and built using lots of bamboo and old flooring and covered with Tiki "stuff." The music is loud, and the mood is festive and fun. It's a refreshing bit of kitsch in a serious, although casual, food scene.

For the PDX audience, Chef Michael Broderick, who is delightful and totally stoked to be cooking in Portland, is working on revamping the menu to include less fried food and more dishes for the many vegetarians who like a strong drink.

Volcano Prawns

(SERVES 3)

6 ounces spicy chile sauce (see recipe below)

1 tablespoon minced garlic

1 tablespoon minced ginger

3 tablespoons peanut oil

½ cup dried wood ear mushroom, thinly sliced

3 cups chow mein egg noodles

2 teaspoons sesame oil

18 large prawns, peeled and deveined

½ red onion, thinly sliced

½ cup white beech mushroom

½ cup edamame, peeled

½ cup cherry tomatoes

2 tablespoons chopped green onions

Special equipment: **Wok**

For the spicy chile sauce: (Makes about 1 cup)

4 ounces sambal oelek (Indonesian chile sauce)

1½ cup oyster sauce

¼ cup Worcestershire sauce

1½ cups ketchup

¼ cup fish sauce

Make the spicy chile sauce.

In a small bowl combine the garlic and ginger with 1 tablespoon peanut oil. Set aside. Soak the wood ear mushrooms in ample water for at least 1 hour. (These steps can also be done a day ahead.)

Blanch the egg noodles for 30 seconds, then toss with sesame oil and reserve.

Be sure the wok is dry before adding the remaining oil. Once the oil is hot and begins to smoke, add the shrimp and toss vigorously.

Then add the garlic and ginger and cook until shrimp are just pink.

Add the remaining ingredients, cook for 45 seconds, and finish with the chile sauce.

Serve over noodles, garnished with green onion.

Combine all ingredients. Can be stored for up to a week or more in the refrigerator.

Higgins

1239 Southwest Broadway
(503) 222-9070
www.HigginsPortland.com
Chef and Owner: Greg Higgins

Greg Higgins, owner and chef of the restaurant that bears his name, has been at the forefront of the farm-to-table movement in Portland way before it became standard operating procedure. Higgins draws a somewhat different demographic than many of the other restaurants that have the same focus and philosophy. It is a business lunch and dinner destination, as serious as that gets in PDX, and it draws theater goers and shoppers in its downtown Portland neighborhood.

With a degree in print making, Higgins had intended to be an artist and worked in kitchens to pay for his education. He found that he felt an enormous sense of satisfaction from cooking and changed paths. Today he is considered to be one of the key players in Portland's extraordinary food scene. He deals exclusively with local farms and suppliers and grows a considerable amount of food that is used in the restaurant.

Higgins butchers a pig on Wednesday and breaks it down and turns it into masterful charcuterie on Thursday. He is devoutly loyal to the ranchers he has been doing business with for years, and he is constantly changing his menu to make way for whatever is fresh and available. As the chef at the Heathman, one of Portland's most stately hotels, for over seventeen years, Higgins developed relationships within the food community that have remained strong throughout his years at the hotel and now seem stronger than ever at his restaurant. The food at Higgins is firmly rooted in the soil and the climate of the Pacific Northwest. Higgins is a man who truly and fully embraces this extraordinary food movement, and he does so with generosity, humility, and commitment.

The panzanella salad starter of roasted beets and spinach with a mint and pea coulis is earthy and fresh, and the oysters with the sweet and spicy ají dulce pepper granita is unique and no less amazing. Being a sucker for all-things pork, I recently ordered the Whole Pig plate—slices of pork loin, sausage, ribs, and braised belly with French green lentils, grilled chicory, and an onion marmalade—which was the envy of everyone else at my table.

ZUPPA DI PESCE

(SERVES 2)

¼ cup olive oil

4 tablespoons minced garlic

1 teaspoon chile flakes

2 tablespoons minced orange zest

1 cinnamon stick

4 cloves

1 onion, peeled and diced ½ inch

3 celery stalks, diced ½ inch

2 carrots, peeled and diced ½ inch

12 ounces peeled, chopped tomatoes

2 cups fish stock

2 cups dry white wine

Salt and pepper to taste

Lemon juice to taste

4 ounces orecchiette or other small-cut pasta

¼ cup olive oil

2 tablespoons minced garlic

1 teaspoon chile flakes

8 ounces halibut, ¾-inch cubes

8 ounces wild salmon, ¾-inch cubes

12 ounces clams or mussels, in shell

8 ounces calamari, cleaned and
    sliced into ½-inch chunks

2 tablespoons olive oil

4 tablespoons minced parsley

Salt and pepper to taste

Lemon juice to taste

In a heavy saucepan heat the olive oil over medium heat. Add the garlic and chile flakes and sauté for 3 to 4 minutes. Add the zest, cinnamon, cloves, onions, celery, and carrots and continue to stir and cook until the onions soften, about 5 to 7 minutes. Stir in the tomatoes, fish stock, and white wine and bring to a simmer. Adjust the seasoning to taste with salt, pepper, and lemon juice and reduce the heat to low.

Bring a pot of water to a simmer and salt it. Begin to cook the pasta. In a large saucepan heat the olive oil over medium-high heat. Add the garlic and chile flakes and stir well. Gently sauté the halibut and salmon in the garlic oil. Add the hot zuppa mixture from step 1 and then the shellfish and calamari. Stir it gently and bring to a simmer.

Check the pasta and drain it when al dente. Season it with olive oil, parsley, and salt and pepper. Adjust the seasoning of the stew with salt and pepper and lemon juice.

To serve, divide the stew into four large bowls. Top with the orecchiette and serve with a crusty loaf of bread and chilled dry white wine.

Victory Bar

3652 Southeast Division Street
(503) 236-8755
www.thevictorybar.com
Chef and Owners: Eric Moore and Yoni Laos

The Victory Bar has special status in Portland. It is the "go to" restaurant for many of Portland's top chefs. The doors open at five every night, and the tables and bar get progressively more crowded as the night unfolds. This restaurant has quite a following, and the owners, Eric Moore and Yoni Laos, do what they do with passion, skill, and artistry.

Eric, originally from Arkansas, started cooking at fifteen in Utah and honed his impressive cooking skills in Switzerland, France, and Belgium. What he brought back to Portland is possibly the most delicious spaetzle east or west of the Rhine. The menu at Victory Bar is small, but it manages to cover all the bases, and there is nothing there that neglects to reflect the high standards of the kitchen. The venison burger is spectacular, as is the pork belly stew and the always vegan soup of the day. There is *poutine*, the wonderful Québécois dish of fries smothered in cheese curds and gravy, and a surprising and terrific sausage po'boy.

Eric's partner, Yoni Laos, reigns behind the bar. The beer selection is renowned, and the cocktails are creative and delightfully drinkable. The propaganda-themed art, including the silk-screened lamps and curtains, reflect Yoni's ongoing love affair with being an artist.

Victory Bar is casual, the menu is eclectic, and it is in a part of town that is quickly becoming a foodie destination. It is my kind of place—casual and warm, comfortable and delicious. When my son and his lovely lady friend came into town—at midnight—we headed right to Victory Bar to hasten their transition from East Coast to West.

CRISPY SPAETZLE & CHEESE

For the caramelized onions:

1 tablespoon butter
1 small white or yellow onion, sliced and julienned
1 bay leaf
Pinch of salt and pepper

For the spaetzle: (Serves 8)

3–4 cups all-purpose flour, sifted*
1 cup sour cream
5 whole large eggs
5 egg yolks
1 tablespoon kosher salt
1 teaspoon ground mace or nutmeg

* Different flours have different weights. The flour used in the restaurant weighs 15 ounces and measures 3 cups. The desired weight is 15 to 16 ounces.

To finish:

4 tablespoons unsalted butter
4 portions of spaetzle dumplings (about 4 cups
     or ½ the batch)
4 tablespoons caramelized onions
1 teaspoon salt
¼ teaspoon black pepper
2 cups heavy cream
1 cup grated gruyère cheese
Bread crumbs or fried crispy onions (for garnish)

To make the onions: In nonstick sauté pan on medium heat, add all ingredients, stirring occasionally until the onions are brown, sweet, and soft (about 10 minutes).

To make the spaetzle: Combine all ingredients in an electric mixing bowl, using paddle attachment on slowest setting. Mix for 3 minutes, then 1 minute on medium speed.

In a large pot (8–10 quarts) bring 5 quarts of water with 1 tablespoon of salt to a boil. Using a spaetzle maker, press the batter through the maker into the water. (Alternatively you can use a slotted spoon and press the mixture through the holes of the spoon into the water.) It is important that there is at least 2 inches in between the maker and the water so the spaetzle can drop into the water and form proper dumplings. If you are quick, you can turn off the heat to reduce the risk of steam burns.

It is recommended that you stir the water twice during this process. Once all of the batter has been pressed, return to high heat, stirring until a full rolling boil is reached and dumplings are puffy and floating on the surface. Strain off the water as you would for any pasta and rinse with cool water. Leave dumplings in strainer to drain any excess water. The dumplings will stay good for 6 days if refrigerated properly.

To finish: In a 14-inch nonstick frying pan, melt butter on medium-high heat, swirling it around to coat the pan. Add spaetzle, evenly distributing as you would for hash browns.

Allow to sit on heat undisturbed for 3 to 4 minutes to brown the first side. Toss dumplings in the pan to mix, then allow to brown once more. While waiting for the second browning, evenly distribute caramelized onions, salt, and pepper. Toss in the pan one more time (or use heat-proof spatula to turn), then add heavy cream. Simmer

cream until slightly thick, add gruyère cheese, and mix until creamy. Remove from heat and serve immediately in desired dish. Top with bread crumbs or fried crispy onions for added texture.

This dish is fantastic with a side of spiced applesauce or roasted apples and pairs well with sausages or roasted game meats.

CUCUMBER VERMOUTH

(YIELDS APPROXIMATELY 1 QUART)

1 whole cucumber, thinly sliced

½ lemon, thinly sliced

Pinch of cardamom, pinch of lavender,
    pinch of chamomile flower

2–3 star anise

24 ounces (3 cups) dry white wine, any variety

4 ounces (8 tablespoons) simple syrup

10 ounces (20 tablespoons) vodka

6–7 sprigs of dill

To make the drink:

2 ounces (4 tablespoons) Dry London gin

1 ounce (2 tablespoons) cucumber vermouth

Olive or pickle (for garnish)

To make the cucumber vermouth: Slice the cucumber as thin as possible. The thinner the slice, the more surface area there is for the cucumber to infuse into the wine.

The amount and type of herbs used is up to personal taste. Feel free to experiment with other fresh or bitter dry herbs and aromatics (for example, orange peel, wormwood, and ginger). The ingredients above should be taken only as a suggestion. Traditionally, vermouth has been a creative process. The basic idea is to improve wine with herbs and sugars.

Place the cucumbers and lemon in a large glass jar. Add the herbs and star anise next, then top off with the wine, simple syrup, and vodka.

Let the mixture sit for 1 week in the glass jar in the refrigerator. Use a very fine strainer to remove the cucumbers and herbs. Let the strained mixture sit overnight. Then pour off the cucumber vermouth into a clean glass bottle, leaving the sediment at the bottom of the jar behind.

Store the final product in the refrigerator for freshness. A suggested recipe:

Make the drink: In a cocktail shaker, rapidly shake the gin and cucumber vermouth with ice until the mixing tin becomes frosty. Strain into a chilled martini glass. Garnish with an olive or pickle.

Try using this cucumber vermouth to make gin and tonics. It helps to add life to boring cocktails.

St. Jack

2039 Southeast Clinton Street
(503) 360-1281
www.Stjackpdx.com
Chef: Aaron Barnett
Owner: Aaron Barnett and Kurt Huffman

There is not a ton of French food in Portland, and what there is tends to lean toward the Paris bistro style. St. Jack, a relative newcomer to town, serves food reflecting the Lyonnaise style of French cooking, with an emphasis on the less high-end cuts of meat and poultry. Its strength lies in making the most of the herbs and flavorings used by the very talented people working the line.

St. Jack's decor is decidedly Paris bistro, with beautifully aged zinc countertops and fantastic white candles all around the room that just drip and drip, cascading down onto the surfaces one would normally try to keep wax-free. They look beautiful and create a tranquil, rustic glow. Chef Aaron Barnett, by birth a Canadian with Scottish parents, describes his folks as the original foodies. He grew up on things like tripe and frogs' legs, and sautéed kidneys for Sunday breakfast. He learned to cook at a young age, though

for part of his formative years he had his heart set on being a veterinarian. He is easygoing, funny, redheaded, and charming, reminiscent of a gentlemanly Louis C.K.

Opening at nine in the morning for great coffee and enticing pastries, this corner restaurant in the lovely Clinton neighborhood has taken off quickly. Pastry Chef Alissa Rozos (formerly of Daniel in New York) makes light and flaky croissants, perfectly caramelized and custardy *canalés,* and simple lunches on crunchy baguettes, including ham and gruyère, plus a truly remarkable quiche. (It might be making a comeback.)

The menu includes such favorites as a Lyonnaise salad of frisée, lardon of bacon, poached egg, and crunchy croutons cooked in bacon fat. The house-made blood sausage with roasted apples and mustard is out of this world, and the steak frites with a rich demi-glace is as good as it gets.

Mussels with Shallots, Garlic, Fennel & Vermouth

(SERVES 2)

2 cups dry white wine

1½ pounds Penn Cove mussels, rinsed and debearded

1 bulb of fennel, remove core and small dice

2 shallots, minced

5 cloves garlic, minced

1 cup vermouth

1 tablespoon Dijon mustard

2 ounces cold unsalted butter

Juice of ½ lemon

2 tablespoons chopped parsley

1 tablespoon chopped tarragon

Black pepper to taste

In a pan large enough to accommodate the mussels, bring the wine to a rolling boil. Add the mussels, fennel, shallots, garlic, and vermouth. Cover with a lid until the mussels begin to open (approximately 3 or 4 minutes).

Remove the open mussels with tongs and transfer to a warm serving bowl. Discard any unopened shells.

Still on high heat, whisk into the mussel broth the Dijon mustard, butter, and lemon juice. Allow the liquid to reduce slightly and finish with the fresh herbs and a good crack of black pepper.

Pour the broth over the mussels. Take the dish outside and enjoy with a baguette and a bottle of dry rosé, and have the best summer night ever.

On my very first visit to Portland, I sat outside at Grand Central Bakery in Multnomah Village for lunch with my friend Janet. There, digging into an unbelievable slice of warm, chocolate Bundt cake on a perfect summer day while watching people pass with their dogs, I fell in love with the city.

For the most part, Portland desserts and pastries seem to fall into the homey category: crisps and cobblers, pies, and all sorts of frozen treats. These include the wonderful almond cake at Navarre, the Random Order pies (all of them!), the roasted strawberry cake at Screen Door, the panna cotta at Nostrana, and the *pudin* at Pambiche. There are, happily, a number of places that veer toward the more formal and equally sublime arena: the savory goat cheese rhubarb galette from Crema and the phyllo-wrapped delight, Shaibeyet from Ya Hala.

Since coffee and tea are huge here, there are lots of choices in every category of sweets. Hazelnut croissants compete with the more standard almond and chocolate, and marionberry Danish are to die for during their short and sweet season. St. Honoré makes it just about impossible to order just one thing; particularly difficult to pass up are the *canelets* and the seasonal bread puddings. From morning to night there are always places to run in and grab a latte and a pastry for the road or to sit and linger over something rich, decadent, and delightful.

Crema Bakery

2728 Southeast Ankeny Street
(503) 234-0206
WWW.CREMABAKERY.COM
Owner: Collin Jones

Crema Bakery is the place I think of whenever someone wants to meet for a cup of coffee. It's not that close to my house (though nothing is ever very far), but it has just the right mood of sunshiny good cheer (even on a cloudy day) and is cozy and totally yummy. If it's early in the morning, I always go for a croissant or the absolutely delicious biscuits with mushrooms and Manchego. These beauties, when warmed quickly, are fantastic. The combination of earthy, cheesy, and flaky makes me crazy. No one can believe how good they are.

At lunchtime I order one of the sandwiches; I especially love the caprese with olives. Nice touch, those olives. The sandwiches never miss with wonderfully combined, slightly warmed fillings on great bread or a savory galette. There are lots of good drink choices—a Spanish latte on a rainy day or an iced Vietnamese coffee when the sun shines.

Manager/owner Collin Jones worked in restaurants starting in his teens in Northern California. The skyrocketing food scene brought him to Portland in 1998, where he attended the Western Culinary Institute. After school, Jones traveled the country cooking on cruise boats and trains for several years before returning to PDX. Jones bought Crema Bakery when it became available in 2011 and has been making deliciousness happen ever since.

Sweet & Savory Galette

(SERVES 8)

For the dough:

2¼ cups all-purpose flour
1¼ stick unsalted butter, chilled and cubed
    (approximately 1-inch pieces)
⅔ teaspoon kosher salt
⅔ teaspoon sugar
½ cup ice cold water
1 egg mixed with water

For the savory goat cheese galette:

2½ cups goat cheese (chevre is ideal)
2½ teaspoons ground fennel
3 stalks of rhubarb, trimmed and split lengthwise,
    sliced on the bias about ¼-inch thick
Salt and pepper to taste

For the pear cream cheese galette:

2½ cups cream cheese, at room temperature
Zest of 1 lemon
3 tablespoons powdered sugar, sifted
1 large egg
2 ripe pears, diced about ½ inch

Combine dry ingredients in a mixer bowl. Add cold, cubed butter and cut in with the paddle attachment of the mixer until butter pieces are about almond size and flour just starts gathering on the walls of the bowl. Stream in cold water and mix until the dough starts coming off the sides of the bowl (10–20 seconds). Do not knead; the dough should seem floury with chunks of butter. Turn the dough out onto a floured work surface, and form it into a 6-inch disk. Wrap it in plastic and refrigerate for 1 hour.

Remove the dough from plastic wrap, dust it with flour, and place it on a well-floured rolling surface. Roll out in multiple directions as you would for a pie. Be generous with the flour; be sure it always feels dry to the touch. Roll until it's just big enough to cut out 8 circles, approximately 5 inches in diameter (a small plate or saucer is usually a good stencil). Stack the rounds on a plate, layering with flour, wrap in plastic, and refrigerate for 30 minutes. Make your filling while this is refrigerating.

Make the savory goat cheese galette: Mix goat cheese and fennel in a medium mixing bowl until well combined. Gently stir in the rhubarb. Add salt and pepper to taste.

Make the pear cream cheese galette: Whip cream cheese with lemon zest, sifted powdered sugar, and the egg until very soft. Gently fold in the diced pears.

To form the galette: Preheat the oven to 350°F. Spread chilled dough rounds out onto your work surface. Scoop approximately 1/3 cup of the filling on to the center of each disk; form into a mound, leaving about 1 inch of dough space around it.

Pinch the edges into eight points around the edge of the dough round; lay the points flat in one direction around the edge.

Brush all exposed dough with a little whisked egg mixed with water. Bake (using a hot pizza/bread stone makes for a lovely crust) for 15 to 20 minutes, until the shell is golden brown.

Cool on a cooling rack or wooden surface.

Navarre

10 Northeast 28th Street
(503) 232-3555
Chef and Owner: John Taboada

John Taboada, owner and chef of the tapas-inspired restaurant Navarre, is all about serving good food without artifice in an intimate setting that is both no-nonsense and romantic. Having worked at many restaurants around PDX, he decided that he wanted his own neighborhood place, a spot to go for reasonable prices, a warm reception, and food that will, at times, border on genius.

Navarre is pocket-size, and the walls are covered with Mason jars filled with house-pickled goodies, wonderful wines from small vineyards, and a number of imported grocery items, each one more interesting than the last. The restaurant serves small and large plates, perfectly suited for sharing, and although the basic theme is Spanish, there are hints of France and Italy running through the daily changing specials. Foie gras on cumin toast is a marvel of both taste and texture. The beet greens roasted with gruyère are outstanding as well.

The restaurant works almost exclusively with a CSA (community-supported agriculture) coalition, and the specials are based on what has been delivered that week

or even that day, combined with the whims and interests of the staff. The group of six who work the kitchen all cover every station, shifting positions to reflect the demands of the current menu and the expertise of the individuals.

Navarre offers a wide selection of flavors and tastes, and it is a treat to be able to enjoy so many different dishes at one sitting, one of the many benefits of the small plate dining style. The restaurant's petite counter displays the wickedly delicious desserts baked in-house. The red velvet and devil's food cakes are terrific, and the almond cake is sublime.

ALMOND CAKE

(SERVES 8–10)

For the cake:

8 ounces almonds (Spanish Marcona work best)
1 cup of sugar
¼ cup all-purpose flour
4 large eggs, room temperature
¼ cup canola oil
¼ cup buttermilk
2 teaspoons lemon zest
Pinch of cinnamon or nutmeg

For the syrup:

1 cup brandy
½ cup sugar

For the ganache:

8 ounces bittersweet chocolate, grated
4 ounces heavy cream

Preheat the oven to 350°F.

Prepare the cake: Cut and place parchment paper in the bottom of a 9-inch pan.

Put the almonds and sugar in a food processor and grind into the flour; don't let the dough overheat or turn to almond butter.

Whip the eggs until light and pale. Mix the oil and buttermilk. Add half the flour, then half the oil mixture, remaining flour, and remaining oil. Add the zest and spice. Pour into the pan. Bake 25 to 30 minutes until the cake tests done.

Make the syrup: Heat the brandy and melt the sugar completely.

When the cake is done and still warm in the pan, pour the syrup over the back of a spoon, and let the cake absorb all the syrup.

Prepare the ganache: Put the grated chocolate in a bowl. Heat the cream until simmering. Pour slowly over the chocolate while stirring. If the chocolate doesn't melt completely, gently place the bowl over a pot of simmering water.

Assemble the cake: Cover the cake with the frosting and let the chocolate set up (frosting hardens and no longer looks wet).

Pambiche

2811 Northeast Glisan Street
(503) 233-0511
www.pambiche.com
Chef and Owner: John Connell Maribona

Cuban cuisine is a fusion of Spanish, African, and Caribbean influences, resulting in a richly flavored and spiced repertoire of dishes, often served with the traditional rice and beans, a main staple of Cuban life. Pambiche is a fun and friendly place to get the best Cuban food in town. It is always busy with patrons who appreciate the terrific spread and the welcoming atmosphere. The restaurant is small, but not in a bad way, and when the weather allows, there is plenty of outside seating.

Owner and chef of the restaurant, charming and warm John Connell Maribona, is Cuban American; he attributes his love of all things culinary to the women in his life. He grew up surrounded by great homemade Cuban cooking and longed for a place where he could offer this treasured cuisine to his hometown.

The offerings at Pambiche are great from start to finish. The delectable taco fritters and codfish and potato croquettes are a fabulous way to start your meal. They are Cuban comfort food, although almost everything on the menu at Pambiche falls into that category. For entrees, there is nothing as soul satisfying as the *ropa vieja* (shredded beef), which translates as "old clothes," or the ajiaco, a stew that is considered by many to be the national dish of Cuba. It is piled high with tropical fruits and vegetables, along with pork and beef.

You need to save room for dessert, though it won't be easy. John's great love is baking, and the desserts and pastries at Pambiche show it. And if you are so inclined, have a pitcher of sangria, a fabulously refreshing explosion of seasonal fruits and flavors.

PUDIN

(SERVES 8–10)

4 cups sugar

¾ cup water

Juice of 1 lime

1 store-bought pound or angel food cake, sliced and
    dried in a 180°F oven for 2 hours and cooled

4 cups whole milk

2 cinnamon sticks

¼ teaspoon salt

1 pound frozen guanábana (soursop)
    (or you can use fresh or canned pears)

1 tablespoon dark rum

12 whole eggs

1½ cups sugar

In a large heavy saucepan, combine the sugar,
water, and lime juice. Cook, simmering, until the
liquid turns dark amber. Immediately turn the
caramel into a 9 x 13-inch baking pan with at least
2-inch sides. At this point the caramel can be set
aside.

Place the cake in a food processor and process
to crumbs. Set aside.

Using a large nonreactive saucepan, heat the
milk, cinnamon sticks, and salt. Scald the mixture
over medium heat until hot. Strain out the
cinnamon sticks.

Puree the fruit and whisk together with the rum,
eggs, and sugar until thoroughly combined,
then strain into the warm milk mixture, stirring
constantly.

Place the cooled cake crumbs into the prepared
baking dish. Pour in the custard and press down
the crumbs to absorb the liquid. Allow to rest for
30 minutes.

Preheat the oven to 350°F. Bake the pudin in a
water bath (a larger dish filled with hot water) for
60 minutes, rotating once or twice during baking.
Check the center of the pudin; if it seems set
and not liquidy, it is done. Allow it to sit at room
temperature and then chill overnight.

When ready to serve, dip the bottom of the
baking dish into warm water for 30 seconds, and
invert onto a serving platter.

Ya Hala

8005 SOUTHEAST STARK STREET
(503) 256-4484
WWW.YAHALARESTAURANT.COM
CHEF AND OWNER: MIRNA ATTAR

The first thing you need to do when you sit down at Ya Hala is order pita bread with either the hummus or baba ghanouj, or both. When the bread arrives it is freshly baked, piping hot and tastes amazing. Hot, just made pita bread with freshly made hummus could be the ultimate comfort food. At Ya Hala, the hummus is smooth and garlicky, the baba ganoush, smoky and earthy. Or order the Shanklish, crumbled white cheese formed into balls, aged, then dusted with thyme-based spices and served on a bed of diced onions, tomatoes, and extra virgin olive oil.

Entrees are not your typical Lebanese fare. Braised succulent pieces of chicken are set upon a mixture of spiced ground beef and basmati rice and garnished with roasted almonds and pine nuts. The extraordinary lamb shank is cooked slowly among bay leaves and other delicate herbs and spices. The meat is tender and the flavor is intense.

Mirna Attar, chef owner of Ya Hala, came to Portland from Lebanon when she was eighteen. Three years into a fine art degree at PSU Mirna got sidetracked, getting married and starting a family. While home with her children Mirna immersed herself in all the cookbooks she could get her hands on. The more complicated the recipe the better.

In 1994, Attar and her husband John bought a Lebanese grocery store in the Montvilla neighborhood of Portland. The store had four tables where people would grab a sandwich or salad and do their shopping. Mirna began cooking there, and before long there were lines out the door, not for the shopping, but for Attar's outstanding dishes. Not able to accommodate their budding clientele, they moved to the grocery store next door, renovated the space, and became Ya Hala, which, by the way, means welcome in Lebanese. Although there is not a large Lebanese community in PDX, Attar's more than forty family members living here make it feel like there is. Attar's three grown kids help out in the restaurant on weekends when they are not at school or at work.

This Lebanese dessert, the cream-filled Shaibeyet, belongs in the dessert hall of fame.

SHAIBEYET WITH CREAM & ROSE WATER SYRUP

(SERVES 6–8)

For the Rose Water Syrup:

Note: This syrup needs time to cool. Prepare accordingly.

1 cup of water
2 cups of sugar
2 tablespoons of fresh squeezed lemon juice
4 tablespoons of rose water

For the Lebanese Cream:

2 cups of heavy cream
2 cups of whole milk
½ cup of sugar
½ cup of cornstarch
4 tablespoons of rose water syrup

1 package of phyllo dough
3 sticks unsalted butter, melted and cooled
5 tablespoons of ground pistachios

Make the syrup: In a medium saucepan, boil 1 cup of water, 2 cups of sugar, and 2 tablespoons of fresh squeezed lemon juice.

Cook on medium until mixture thickens and develops a yellow tint. Turn off heat. Stir in 4 tablespoons of rose water.

Place in refrigerator until very cold, approximately 2 hours.

Make the cream: Mix all of the top ingredients together until the starch is completely dissolved. In a medium saucepan cook the mixture on medium heat until the cream thickens.

Pour mixture into a shallow bowl and cover with wax paper. Place in the refrigerator for about two hours (or until very cold).

Heat oven to 350°F.

Fold and bake the pastry: Unroll the phyllo dough package and lay flat on the table. Separate one layer of phyllo dough (this will be a very thin piece) and lay it flat on the table. Fold it in half lengthwise, then fold in half again.

Place 1½ tablespoons of the Lebanese cream centered; about 2 inches from the bottom. Fold the right bottom corner over the cream and lay it flat on the opposite side. This should create a triangle shape. Take the remaining left corner and fold upwards. The left corner should still be on the left side of the dough. Take the left corner again and fold to the right. Continue this folding pattern until you reach the end of the dough.

Melt 3 sticks of butter and place in a medium-size bowl.

Dip each piece of the folded Shaibeyet into the melted butter. Place on a cookie sheet 2½ inches apart.

Bake on the middle rack of the preheated oven until golden brown. This should take 15–20 minutes.

Place directly onto your serving dish and drizzle the cold rose water syrup over it.

Garnish with ground pistachios.

St. Honoré

2335 Northwest Thurman Street
(503) 445-4342
www.sainthonorebakery.com
Head Baker/Owner: Dominique Geulin

St. Honoré has two locations, one in the fashionable northwest neighborhood, the other in the town of Lake Oswego, just outside Portland (315 1st Street, Lake Oswego, OR 97034; 503-445-1379). Although they draw a very different crowd, both places offer outstanding breads and pastries, light and fresh soups, interesting French salads, and hot and cold sandwiches. The Portland shop gets a constant flow of people meeting for a meal or sitting and sipping a wonderful latte while reading, texting, or living the PDX life. There are both individual and communal tables, and there is definitely a Francophile feel. The boulangerie is open and airy with floor-to-ceiling windows. The flagstone floor and thick wooden tables evoke images of the French countryside, and the smell of fresh-baked bread fills every nook of this neighborhood bakery. And even if you think you are just going to get a mocha, I guarantee you will pick up something else as well.

The pastries are what St. Honoré is known for, and there is no question that they are wonderful. The fantastic and unusual treat called *chouquettes* are addictively delicious puffy baked pastry balls made with a *pâte à choux* and sprinkled with rock sugar and served in a little paper bag. The orange gâteau is moist and fragrant, the strawberry napoleon is wonderful, and the glorious *canalé* is caramelized, vanilla, chewy goodness. The pastries reflect the seasons: an amazing bread pudding with apples in the fall and a great *bûche de Noël* during the holidays. Berries rule the show in the summer. On a rainy day, it is a cozy place, and in the sun, sitting outside at little tables, you are transported to Paris.

ALMOND PEAR TART

(SERVES 8–10)

It is important to let the tart rest after covering the surface with sugar before baking. This process, along with the sprinkled almond slices, creates a thin top crust with a crunchy texture, which is unique to this tart.

½ cup sugar
1 cup water
1 large Bartlett pear*
½ vanilla bean, split and scraped

*Can be substituted with a canned pear.

For the almond batter:

½ cup granulated sugar
⅓ cup almond meal
4 large eggs
1 drop almond extract
2 tablespoons pear poaching liquid**
Frozen puff pastry, good quality
Almond batter (see recipe below)
Granulated sugar
Sliced almonds

**Substitute with juice from canned pears.*

In a small saucepan dissolve the sugar in water to make a simple syrup.

Peel, halve, and core a pear. Poach the pear in the simple syrup by simmering over low heat with the vanilla beans (pod and beans) until soft. Let cool.

Make the almond batter: Combine sugar and almond meal in a bowl.

Beat the eggs and add them to the dry mix. Stir until fully dissolved. Add the almond extract and pear liquid and stir well.

Prepare the tart: Preheat the oven to 350°F. Use a 9-inch tart tin with a removable bottom. Allow the puff pastry to defrost according to the directions on the package. Form the dough into the tin and crown the rim with a little edge of dough.

Line the tart shell with parchment paper and fill with beans or pie weights. Prebake the shell in the oven for 15 to 20 minutes until set and light golden on the bottom. Let the shell cool. Remove the beans.

Chop the poached pear to ½-inch size and place on the bottom of the shell. Pour almond batter over pears to just below the rim of the shell.

Sprinkle a generous amount of granulated sugar to cover the top surface, and let rest to form a film, for about 15 to 20 minutes.

Scatter sliced almonds over the surface of the tart. Bake for about 30 to 35 minutes until the center is firm to the touch.

Allow to cool before removing from tart tin.

Note: The dough in the following recipe can be used instead of the frozen puff pastry.

FOOD PROCESSOR QUICK PIE/TART DOUGH

1½ cups flour
1 tablespoon sugar
¼ teaspoon salt
10 tablespoons unsalted butter
2 teaspoons vinegar
½ cup ice water

Combine flour, sugar, salt, and butter in a sealable plastic bag and freeze completely. (This may be done up to 3 months in advance.)

Mix vinegar and ice water in a bowl.

Turn the contents of the freezer bag into a food processor; pulse until chunks of butter are the size of large peas.

Add vinegar mixture to flour mixture and pulse briefly just to incorporate. Form the dough into a disk, cover with plastic wrap, and refrigerate for at least 1 hour or overnight.

On a well-floured surface, roll dough out to 1/8-inch thick. Fit into pie/tart pan and cut away excess dough. Cover and chill for 1 hour.

Preheat the oven to 400°F. Prick the bottom of the shell with a fork; line the shell with foil and fill with dried beans. Bake the shell for 10 minutes. Remove the beans and foil and bake the shell until light brown, about 10 minutes more. Let cool before filling.

Screen Door

2337 East Burnside Street
(503) 542-0880
WWW.SCREENDOORRESTAURANT.COM
Owners: David and Nicole Mouton
Chef: Rick Widmayer
Baker: Erin Eberlein-Sage

Whenever people visit us from out of town, we inevitably head to one of the most soul-nourishing eateries in Portland: Screen Door. I always assume that everyone—with the exclusion of vegetarians and vegans—has a constant craving for perfectly fried chicken. Perhaps I am projecting, but I don't think so. Screen Door's awesome chicken, crispy and tender, along with outstanding jambalaya and melt-in-your-mouth brisket, draws people from all over town to this welcoming destination that is so comfortable and friendly you'll want to come back again and again. And when you return, you will be remembered and made to feel at home.

One of the draws of this hugely successful restaurant is the frequently changing menu of seasonal farmers' market offerings: creative and fresh salads such as strawberry and pluot (a hybrid of plum and apricot), or beets and Romaine with grapefruit, oranges, pistachios, and goat cheese.

Brunch is served on weekends, and the fried chicken and waffles dish is legendary. So are the Eggs Sardou, the maple bacon waffles, and the grits. With a cup of coffee, or the southern-style lightly sweetened ice tea or lemonade, you can't go wrong.

As hard as it may be to think about eating dessert after such a satisfying and hearty

meal, it is not to be missed. Pastry Chef Erin Eberlein-Sage is turning out some of the best biscuits, pies, and cakes in Portland. The old standby southern dessert requirement, pecan pie, has a not-too-sweet flavor and delectable crust. Other choices are equally gratifying. The dark chocolate and peanut butter stack (devil's food cake with peanut butter mousse, peanut crunch, and dark chocolate ganache), served with homemade peanut butter ice cream, and the Bartlett pear crisp with oat, coconut, and almond topping, served warm with homemade buttermilk caramel ice cream, are both too good to miss.

ROASTED STRAWBERRY & COCONUT CAKE
WITH COCONUT ICE CREAM

(SERVES 10–12)

For the strawberry cake:

2⅓ cup all-purpose flour

2 teaspoons baking powder

1 teaspoon salt

½ cup buttermilk

½ cup milk

1 teaspoon vanilla bean paste

2 teaspoons coconut rum

1 teaspoon grated lemon zest

1 cup unsalted butter, room temperature

1½ cups sugar

3 large eggs

3 cups small strawberries, quartered (from 1½ pints)

For the roasted strawberries: (Yields approximately 2 cups roasted berries, enough for 1 cake plus some extra)

1½ pints small strawberries, washed and hulled

For the strawberry syrup: (Yields approximately ¾ cup)

½ cup sugar

½ cup water

All juice from bowl of roasted strawberries
(can spoon out; it will be thick)

For the whipped cream frosting (Yields frosting for 1 9-inch-round three-layer cake):

3 cups heavy whipping cream, cold

½ cup powdered sugar

1 teaspoon vanilla paste

1 tablespoon coconut rum

3 cups sweetened flaked coconut, for decorating cake

Preheat the oven to 350°F. Grease three 9-inch-round cake pans and line with parchment paper. Sift together flour, baking powder, and salt and set aside. Stir together both milks, vanilla, coconut rum, and lemon zest and set aside.

In a standing mixer, cream together the butter and sugar until nearly white and fluffy. Add eggs one at a time. Alternate adding the milk and flour mixtures, mixing well between each addition: ⅓ flour, ½ milk, ⅓ flour, ½ milk, ⅓ flour. Gently fold in strawberries. Pour the batter into the pans, then spread with spatula to even. Bake for 20 minutes, rotate cakes, and bake for 10 to 15 minutes more, until toothpick tests clean.

Cakes will fall slightly. Remove the cakes in the pan to a cooling rack for 10 minutes. Run a small knife around the edge of the pan, turn out onto a rack, peel off the parchment, and let cool.

Roast the strawberries: Preheat the oven to 400° F. Slice the strawberries ⅓-inch thick. Spread in an even layer in a shallow roasting pan. Cook for 15 to 20 minutes, until softened and slightly shriveled. Place the berries and any berry juice in a small bowl. Cover and chill until cold.

Make the syrup: Heat sugar and water in a small pan to boiling. Let boil until clear, a few seconds. Pour into a small bowl. Stir in the strawberry juice. Chill until cold.

Make the cream: Whip cream, powdered sugar, vanilla, and rum until stiff.

To assemble: Put one layer of the cake facedown on a serving dish. Brush lightly with some of the strawberry syrup. Spread a thin layer of frosting over the cake. Staying 1 inch from the edge of the cake, make a single layer of roasted strawberries on frosting. Cover with another thin layer of frosting, sealing the edge well. Top with another layer of cake. Repeat syrup, frosting, strawberries, frosting, and final cake layer. Brush the top layer of cake with syrup.

Spread a generous layer of frosting on the top and sides of the cake. Lightly press coconut flakes onto the sides and top of the cake, being sure to cover well. Let chill for 1 hour to set.

Serve with strawberry sauce, diced strawberries, and toasted coconut ice cream.

MINT JULEP

(MAKES 1 COCKTAIL)

Fresh mint, muddled
2 ounces (4 tablespoons) bourbon
1 teaspoon simple syrup
2 ounces (4 tablespoons) soda water (club soda)

In a shaker combine the mint, bourbon, and simple syrup with ice. Shake and pour into a glass. Top with a splash of soda water.

RANDOM ORDER

800 NORTHEAST ALBERTA STREET
(971) 340-6995
OWNER: TRACY OLSON

My first experience at Random Order was unplanned. I was dining with a friend from Kansas, who mentioned that she had just eaten a slice of pie at Random Order, a pie that was as good as her grandmother's, the long-standing pie queen of Hiawatha. We declined the dessert menu where we were eating and headed to Random Order on Alberta Street. We were a group of five and had a hard time choosing between the nine different pies in the case. The six slices we settled on—the three cream pies, the triple berry, the salted caramel apple, and the mouthwatering blueberry rhubarb pie—were perfection, made lovingly with the first fruit of the season. This is not unusual at Random Order, where nothing but the freshest seasonal ingredients are used in everything they make. The bakery has a homey vibe, with mismatched tables and chairs of all heights and sizes. It is in the super-funky Alberta neighborhood, and at times there are actually crowds hanging out on the street sipping latte and just chilling out.

Owner Tracy Olson came to open Random Order through a circuitous route that included a law degree from Lewis & Clark College and some time in the not-for-profit sector studying the bull trout, while she dreamed of starting an art studio for kids combined with a coffee shop. She was advised to start with the coffee shop, and it has now been here for over a decade, with a steady stream of customers bringing books or laptops, taking advantage of the free Internet, and loving everything on the Random Order menu.

BLUEBERRY RHUBARB PIE

(SERVES 6–8)

This simple lattice-topped blueberry rhubarb pie should rest in the freezer before baking, one of the secrets of Grandma's kitchen.

To make flaky pastry crusts: (Yields 2 crusts)

2 cups plus 2 tablespoons pastry flour

1 teaspoon baking powder

1 teaspoon salt

1 tablespoon sugar

3½ tablespoons unsalted butter, cubed in uniform pieces and chilled in the freezer

5–8 tablespoons ice water

1 tablespoon apple cider vinegar

For the filling:

¾ cup granulated sugar

Zest of 1 orange

¼ teaspoon salt

¼ teaspoon cinnamon

¼ cup cornstarch

4 cups rhubarb, chopped in 1½-inch pieces

Heavy cream (to brush on pie top)

Sanding sugar (to dust)

Note: Keep your ingredients cold, and don't overwork them.

Make the crust: Measure flour, baking powder, salt, and sugar into food processor bowl. Pulse briefly to combine. Add butter and pulse until the butter is pea size and the dough resembles a coarse meal.

Transfer to a mixing bowl. Add 5 tablespoons ice water and vinegar. Toss with your hands, kneading the dough together until just combined, being careful not to overwork. Add up to 3 tablespoons more ice water if the dough is dry and not holding together.

Divide into two equal parts, wrap with plastic wrap, and press into 5- to 6-inch disks. Cool in the refrigerator for at least 1 hour.

Make the filling: Combine the sugar and zest in a large bowl. Add salt, cinnamon, and cornstarch; mix well, then add the rhubarb and blueberries, tossing it all together. Let this fruit mix sit for at least 15 minutes.

To assemble the pie: On a lightly floured surface roll out one bottom crust to ¼-inch thick and line a shallow 9-inch pie dish. Trim excess pastry, leaving about 1 inch overhang. Pour your fruit filling into the pie dish and refrigerate while you do your lattice top.

Roll out the second disk to a ¼-inch circle. Carefully cut the dough into 4-inch strips with a scalloped pastry wheel or sharp knife.

Moisten the rim of the pie with a small amount of water. Lay the first two lattices in the same direction, about 2 inches apart from one another.

Now lift one of the strips, and lay down the third dough strip in the opposite direction as the first two.

Now lay the first dough strip back down. This will result in the third dough strip lying underneath one strip, and over the top of the other. Repeat this step with the final dough strip.

Tuck lattice strips and crimp. Chill in the freezer for 20 minutes.

Preheat the oven to 400°F. Line a sheet pan with tinfoil to catch any pie drippings and place on the rack beneath the pie. Brush the pie with heavy cream and sprinkle it with sanding sugar. Cover with a piece of vented foil.

Bake in the preheated oven for 30 minutes. At 30 minutes, reduce the oven heat to 350°F, remove the foil, and rotate. Bake for 30 minutes more.

About 25 minutes later you should be smelling deliciousness, and the filling should be starting to bubble. Check the bottom, rotate the pie, and check that it is browning nicely.

Continue baking, checking the pie every 10 minutes to see that the bottom is browned and the filling is bubbling. It may take 20 to 30 minutes more.

Take the pie out of the oven when the bottom is golden brown. Let cool for 1½ hours.

Grand Central Bakery

MULTIPLE LISTINGS
www.GrandCentralBakery.com
CO-OWNER/CUISINE DIRECTOR: PIPER DAVIS

Both Portland and Seattle are hosts to the chain Grand Central Bakery, with four shops in Portland and two in Seattle. The number of locations is a stroke of good fortune for anyone who gets to live near one. Co-owner Piper Davis has a kind of earth mother charm, and the unpretentious shops feel very Northwest in style and atmosphere, complete with outdoor seating and birds hovering for a crumb or two.

The breakfast sandwiches, like the egg sandwich with bacon, cheese, and store-made tomato jam, are luscious; lunch offerings, especially the made-from-scratch soups, are amazing and perfect on rainy Portland days, and the bread is among the best in town. Grand Central Bakery breads are served at many of the restaurants in Portland, and it was great news for Portlanders when the bakery began selling its own puff pastry and pie dough as well as assembled pies that you buy frozen and bake at home, which makes it possible to have a terrific marionberry pie at Thanksgiving.

The cakes, cookies, and homey pastries when paired with the Stumptown coffee are all terrific. The cowboy cookie, a chewy combo of an oatmeal and chocolate chip, is irresistible. The chocolate cake is deep flavored and moist, and the hand pies with various fruit fillings are magnificent.

One of the best parts? Grand Central offers cute bag lunches, complete with a sandwich, a bag of chips, and a cookie. I feel like a happy kid every time I order one.

Nectarine Tart

(SERVES 8)

Both the filling and crust can be made ahead of time for this simple summer tart. Although nectarine is my favorite way to go, this recipe works well with any stone fruit. Try apricots with this recipe—it's divine.

1¼ cups all-purpose flour

1 tablespoon sugar

1 teaspoon salt

1 stick (4 ounces) butter

3–4 tablespoons water

1 teaspoon lemon juice

1½ pounds (3 or 4) whole ripe nectarines

¼ cup honey

¼ cup sugar

2 tablespoons cornstarch

2 tablespoons lemon juice

½ teaspoon vanilla

Egg wash (to brush crust)

Granulated sugar (for garnish)

Chill the flour, sugar, and salt in a mixing bowl for at least 2 hours or up to overnight. Dice the butter into ½-inch cubes and toss with the flour. Fill a drinking glass with ice and cold water. Squeeze 1 tablespoon lemon juice into liquid measure. Add the cold water to the lemon juice right before pouring it into the pie dough. Be careful not to add any of the cubes or chunks of ice.

Use your forefingers and thumbs to rub the butter with the chilled dry ingredients. Press the cube of butter into a flat chip with each movement. It should be cold enough that you're coating the butter pieces with the flour. Stop mixing when the texture of the flour changes from silky to mealy.

Use a fork to make a well in the flour mixture. Drizzle ¾ of the cold water with lemon juice in as you gradually pull the dry ingredients into the middle with the fork, mixing gently. Check the hydration of the dough by gathering a small fistful; if it holds together, it's ready. If it is dry or crumbly, mix a little longer before adding more water, 1 tablespoon at a time, aiming for dry spots.

When the dough has the proper amount of water, it will come together with minimal effort and no deliberate packing. Form the dough into a disk, gathering and pressing with the palms of your hands, keeping in mind that you are building horizontal layers for flakiness. My favorite way to do this is on a piece of plastic. I use the wrap itself to pull the dough in tight and contain any dry floury spots; then hydrate further by continuing to absorb the liquid as the dough rests in the refrigerator.

It's important to chill the dough again at this point, before attempting to roll. Time in the refrigerator ensures that the butter does not warm up and allows the dough to relax. Beginners should let the dough chill for at least 1 to 2 hours, or it can sit in the refrigerator several days before you use it. More experienced pie bakers will know when to hurry things up a bit, but always return the dough to rest and chill if you are having trouble rolling it.

Pit and slice nectarines with skin on. Add honey and sugar and gently toss to combine. Make a slurry with the cornstarch and lemon juice and stir into fruit. Cook while stirring mixture over low to medium heat until mixture bubbles and nectarines begin to break down. The filling

will look shiny and begin to thicken when it is ready. Remove from heat and add vanilla. Cool completely before using.

On a lightly floured surface, roll dough into 14- to 15-inch-diameter circle, ⅛ inch thick. Fold circle in half and in half again, and transfer it to a baking sheet lined with parchment paper, centering the point. Unfold dough and gently spread fruit or spread filling (there should be about 1½ cups) over pastry, leaving a 3-inch border all the way around. Carefully lift and fold the edge of dough over the fruit. Allow the dough to pleat each time you lift it. It should pleat about 8 to 10 times as you work your way around. If you have time, chill the tart for 20 minutes.

Preheat the oven to 350°F. For a shiny, sweet finish, lightly brush with egg wash and sprinkle with sugar. Bake in the middle of the oven until pastry is golden brown and fruit is soft and bubbly, 45 to 55 minutes. Rotate the pan once during baking, after about 25 minutes.

Lovejoy Bakers

939 Northwest 10th Avenue
(503) 208-3113
www.Lovejoybakers.com
Co-Owners: Marc and Tracy Frankel
Head Baker/Co-Owner: Dan Griffin

In what may be the heart of the Pearl District, the light-filled Lovejoy Bakers is making a name for itself in a tough town to make your mark. The bakery serves spectacular sandwiches, a personal favorite being the roast beef with caramelized onions and cheddar with a nice slather of horseradish aioli. And the cream of tomato soup with a grilled cheddar and Fontina sandwich is crusty on the outside and heaven on the inside.

Lovejoy offers a combo of excellent baguettes and ciabatta rolls, as well as hard-to-find breads, like a kaiser roll and rye bread with caraway seeds. Being from New York, one of the things that I have missed is a good buttered kaiser with my coffee in the morning. The poppy seed–coated roll from Lovejoy has happily ended my search.

Beyond breads, the pastries, from the Danish to the twisted, flaky, and heavenly cinnamon braids coated with cinnamon sugar, are excellent and perfect for dunking. Cookies, like the pumpkin with brown butter frosting studded with currants and walnuts and the triple chocolate, are rich and chewy. Traffic flows through the bakery pretty much all day, and its selection of day-old breads and pastries fly off the shelf. Just last week, for instance, I made a very good bread pudding with the day-old almond croissants.

The smell of good bread baking, like the sound of lightly flowing water is indescribable in its evocation of innocence and delight. MFK FISHER

Chocolate Sandwich Cookie

(MAKES 30–36 COOKIES)

2 cups unsalted butter

2 cups sugar

4 large eggs

5 cups all-purpose flour

1 cup unsweetened cocoa powder

1 teaspoon salt

2 teaspoons vanilla extract

For the easy buttercream filling:

1 cup butter, softened

3–4 cups powdered sugar

¼ teaspoon salt

1 tablespoon vanilla extract or 1 vanilla bean,
    split and scraped

1–4 tablespoons milk

1 cup melted dark chocolate

Preheat the oven to 375°F. Cream the butter and sugar in a bowl. Beat in the eggs one at a time until combined. Sift the flour, cocoa powder, and salt together and set aside in a bowl. Add the flour mixture in 2 to 3 additions, scraping the bowl in between each addition.

Once all of the flour has been incorporated, cover the dough in plastic wrap and allow it to chill for at least 30 minutes.

Roll the dough to ¼-inch thickness and cut with any shape cookie cutter you like. Bake the cookies on parchment-lined baking sheets until done, about 7 to 9 minutes. Allow to cool.

Make the filling: With a standing or handheld mixer, beat the butter for 2 to 3 minutes on medium speed. Add 3 cups of powdered sugar on low speed until incorporated. Turn the speed to medium and add vanilla extract (or bean scrapings if using), salt, and 2 tablespoons of

milk and beat for 2 to 3 minutes. If too stiff, add more milk.

When the cookies have cooled, spread half the cookies with the filling and top. Dip half the cookie in the melted chocolate and lay on a rack or parchment paper for the chocolate to set.

Nostrana

1401 Southeast Morrison Street
(503) 234-2427
www.Nostrana.com
Chef and Owner: Cathy Whims

Intensely regional Italian food, thin-crust wood oven pizza, and a challenging menu make Chef-Owner Cathy Whims's restaurant, Nostrana, a place where you know you will always get a great, authentic meal. With an exposed wood ceiling, tons of windows, and some interesting art on the wall, Nostrana has a comfortable and contented feel.

It is the kind of restaurant that goes both ways. It is a great place to drop by, sit at the counter facing the large and frequently stocked wood oven, and enjoy a great beer and an even better pizza with perfect crust and the freshest toppings—a terrific quick meal. Or if you are looking for something more elaborate, perhaps romantic, Nostrana can do that, too. The tables are carefully arranged so they're not too close to each other, and the staff is professional and knowledgeable. Upon entering, you immediately feel at ease, and although the food is sophisticated, there is nothing stuffy about the place. The menu allows you to have a *paglia e fieno* (straw and hay) (a spinach and egg fettuccine with Oregon shrimp and chile flakes, garlic, and cream) or the tenderest pork chop, with tomato salsa and braised greens. If it's a great piece of beef you're craving, the ridiculously good *bistecca fiorentina* is a 2-inch rib steak aged fifty days.

With her wonderful, positive energy, Cathy Whims is clearly passionate about her work. She grew up and went to school in Chapel Hill, North Carolina, with parents who loved to cook and eat good food. Whims worked for years catering and making private dinners in Chapel Hill, before heading to the Bay Area to work in some impressive

kitchens. She came to Portland in 1979, rotated through all the stations of the famed Italian restaurant Genoa, and eventually became one of its owners.

Whims opened Nostrana in 2006 and has fiercely committed to the area's farmers and ranchers. She has dedicated herself to serving pure and unaffected food that is not overpowering, but that also goes great with a glass or two of wine.

PANNA COTTA

(SERVES 6)

1 tablespoon unflavored, powdered gelatin
3 tablespoons water
1 cup heavy cream
½ cup sugar
1 cup whole milk yogurt

In a small bowl sprinkle gelatin over 3 table-spoons water and let soften for 3 minutes without stirring.

In a heavy saucepan over low heat, warm cream with sugar. Remove from heat and stir in gelatin. Gradually whisk in the yogurt.

Lightly coat 6 individual 4-ounce ramekins with an unflavored vegetable oil. Pour in cream mixture and refrigerate overnight.

To serve, run the knife around the edge of a ramekin, turn the ramekin upside down on a dessert plate, and shake downward sharply once (or twice) to release the panna cotta.

Skin & Bones Bistro

5425 East Burnside Street
(503) 236-3610
www.skinandbonesbistro.com
Chef and Owner: Caleb McBee

If I had to guess what the smallest full-service restaurant in Portland is, Skin & Bones would most definitely be a contender. The setting is a little room in a little house on the east side of town. The room is absolutely without glitz or glamour. It feels as though it could have existed one hundred years ago. There is definitely something charming about how completely unpretentious this place is.

The chef, Caleb McBee, looks like he just stepped off the farm. He is warm and friendly and makes you feel as if he is feeding you in his home. In fact, McBee lives next door, and his herb and vegetable garden supplies the majority of products used in his cooking. That is so Portland.

The menu is small and changes weekly. The vegetable dishes shine. The roasted cauliflower with a roasted garlic aioli is crunchy creamy with a little kick of spice, and roasted Padrón peppers are full of their deep, earthy flavor. Other main entrees are impressive as well, with the confit of pork belly and the chef's toast, which changes constantly, worthy offerings.

One of the best dessert choices is the buttermilk pie, served with compote of macerated fresh cherries. The tangy buttermilk flavor with the sweet cherries will win you over. In the fall, try the pumpkin pie made with Cinderella pumpkins—it will knock your sneakers off. It is the best pumpkin pie I have ever had.

PUMPKIN PIE

(SERVES 8)

2 eggs
1½ cups pumpkin puree
1 cup brown sugar
1 cup cream
1 teaspoon cinnamon
½ teaspoon nutmeg
½ teaspoon ground ginger
Favorite single pie crust

Heat oven to 350°F. In a large bowl beat the eggs and sugar together. Beat until the sugar is fully incorporated.

Add all the remaining ingredients, excluding the crust, and beat until well mixed.

Line a prepared pan with the crust. Pour mixture into the pie shell and bake until set, about 45–50 minutes. The filling will rise and then settle when cooling. The pie is light and luscious.

Metric U.S. Approximate Equivalents

LIQUID INGREDIENTS

Metric	U.S. Measures	Metric	U.S. Measures
1.23 ml	¼ tsp.	29.57 ml	2 tbsp.
2.36 ml	½ tsp.	44.36 ml	3 tbsp.
3.70 ml	¾ tsp.	59.15 ml	¼ cup
4.93 ml	1 tsp.	118.30 ml	½ cup
6.16 ml	1¼ tsp.	236.59 ml	1 cup
7.39 ml	1½ tsp.	473.18 ml	2 cups or 1 pt.
8.63 ml	1¾ tsp.	709.77 ml	3 cups
9.86 ml	2 tsp.	946.36 ml	4 cups or 1 qt.
14.79 ml	1 tbsp.	3.79 l	4 qts. or 1 gal.

DRY INGREDIENTS

Metric	U.S. Measures	Metric	U.S. Measures
2 (1.8) g	1/16 oz.	80 g	2⅘ oz.
3½ (3.5) g	⅛ oz.	85 (84.9) g	3 oz.
7 (7.1) g	¼ oz.	100 g	3½ oz.
15 (14.2) g	½ oz.	115 (113.2) g	4 oz.
21 (21.3) g	¾ oz.	125 g	4½ oz.
25 g	⅞ oz.	150 g	5¼ oz.
30 (28.3) g	1 oz.	250 g	8⅞ oz.
50 g	1¾ oz.	454 g	1 lb. (16 oz.)
60 (56.6) g	2 oz.	500 g	1 livre (17⅗ oz.)

Glossary

Baton: A batonette cut is a thick matchstick size, 3 inches long and ¼ inch thick. This shape and size hold up well to cooking.

Béchamel sauce: Also known as white sauce, it is one of the mother sauces of French cuisine and is used in many recipes of Italian cuisine, for example lasagne.

Beurre Monté: Refers to melted butter that remains emulsified, even at temperatures higher than that at which butter usually breaks. In order to make a beurre monté, you need to boil a very small quantity of water, i.e., 1 to 4 tablespoons. Once water has come to a boil, turn the heat down and start whisking the cold butter into the water, one or two chunks at a time. Add more butter whenever the chunks have melted. Once the emulsion is started, more butter can be added at a time. Continue adding butter while whisking until one has the desired quantity of beurre monté. The beurre monté must then be held warm, but under 190°F or else it will break.

Brunoise: Basic knife cut measuring ⅛ × ⅛ × ⅛ inch.

Chiffonade: A cooking technique in which herbs or leafy vegetables (such as Swiss chard and spinach) are cut into long, fine strips. This is generally accomplished by stacking leaves, rolling them tightly, then cutting across the rolled leaves with a sharp knife, producing thin ribbons.

Clarified butter: Milk fat rendered from butter to separate the milk solids and water from the butterfat. Typically, it is produced by melting butter and allowing the different components to separate by density. The water evaporates, some solids float to the surface and are skimmed off, and the remainder of the milk solids sink to the bottom and are left behind when the butter fat (which would then be on top) is poured off.

Confit: A cooking term for a variety of foods, most often meats, preserved by being salted and cooked slowly in their own fat. Confit can also be a condiment of fruit or vegetables cooked to the consistency of jam. In addition to meats, confit refers to other foods, including garlic or lemons, cooked and preserved in oil or lard in a similar method.

Cure; curing: Curing is the process of preserving food, particularly meat or fish, by the addition of salt, nitrates, or sugar or by smoking. Food dehydration was the earliest form of curing.

Dice: Dice means to cut foods into small ¼-inch squares. These pieces should be as even as possible, usually for appearance. In some cuisines, especially Southeast Asian, exact sizes are important for even cooking.

Julienne: Foods that have been cut into thin, matchstick strips. The food is first cut into ⅛-inch-thick slices. The slices are stacked, then cut into ⅛-inch-thick strips. The strips may then be cut into whatever length is desired.

Lardons: The French use this word to refer to bacon that has been diced, blanched, and fried.

Liqueur: An alcoholic beverage that has been flavored with fruit, herbs, nuts, spices, flowers, or cream and bottled with added sugar.

Macerate: Raw, dried, or preserved fruits or vegetables softened by soaking in liquid. This technique makes food more flavorful and tender.

Mandoline: A metal cooking utensil used for slicing and for cutting juliennes. This tool once was relegated to professional kitchens only but has gained popularity among home cooks. There are plastic versions available for considerably less money.

Mince: To cut food into very small pieces. Minced food is smaller than chopped food.

Pistou: A cold sauce made from cloves of garlic, basil, and olive oil. Some more modern versions of the recipe include grated Parmesan or similar hard cheeses.

Render: To melt animal fat over low heat so that it separates from any connective pieces of tissue, which, during rendering, turn brown and crisp and are generally referred to as cracklings.

Rondeau: A wide, round pot that is relatively shallow, usually with two handles. It is generally made of stainless steel.

Roux: French for "reddish brown," a roux is a thickener for sauces and soups that combines equal parts flour and butter.

Sweat: To cook over low heat in a small amount of fat, usually in a covered pan or pot. Often used to describe the way aromatic vegetables such as onions, carrots, and celery are cooked prior to adding other ingredients. The objective in sweating vegetables is to soften them and release the moisture in them, not to brown them. This release of moisture is how the term "sweat" gets its name.

Temper: It means to bring the temperature of the egg mixture up closer to the temperature of the hotter ingredients you will be mixing it with to prevent the egg from cooking.

Vegan: A person who avoids using or consuming animal products. While vegetarians choose not to use flesh foods, vegans also avoid dairy and eggs, as well as fur, leather, wool, down, and cosmetics or chemical products tested on animals.

Water bath, or bain marie: Cooking technique that consists of placing a smaller container of food in a large, shallow pan of warm water, which surrounds the food with gentle heat. The food may be cooked in this manner either in an oven or on top of a stove. This technique is designed to cook delicate dishes such as custards, sauces, and savory mousses without breaking or curdling them as a result of too high or direct heat. It can also be used to keep cooked foods warm.

Index

About the Author

Laurie Goldrich Wolf has been making, eating, or writing about food professionally for over twenty years. After attending the Culinary Institute of America, she worked as a chef and caterer in New York and Vermont. Laurie married the extraordinarily talented photographer Bruce Wolf and changed gears to become a food stylist for magazines. Food styling led to writing for magazines, and Laurie acted as the food editor for *Mademoiselle* and *Child* magazines, writing original recipes as well as styling many others.

During this journey Laurie and Bruce raised a couple of lovely children, Nick and Olivia, and Laurie turned her focus to cookbooks and craft books.

Laurie credits a move to Portland, Oregon, in 2008 as one of the best decisions she's ever made, with both Laurie and Bruce captivated by the amazing food and drink scene. Getting to know the bright and creative people in the Portland food business and working on this book together has been a blast, and a combined weight gain of more pounds than they will ever admit is the unfortunate proof.